Hand in Hand

Hand in Hand

A Biography of Doctors Daniel and Lauretta Kress

By

PEARLE PEDEN

Southern Publishing Association

Nashville, Tennessee

Table of Contents

Lovingly Dedicated to
My Sons

Phillip
Donald
Roger

Mr. Seventeen

$\mathcal{M}$R. SEVENTEEN" stood before his older brother, pleading for a favor.

"But, John, it's my last chance to meet her. She's going home tomorrow." His words were weighted with urgency. "Besides, she's more my age than yours, and I have the phaeton all washed and shined."

That should do it. John knew what a job it was to shine the family carriage. Dan looked almost comical, standing there in his work clothes, still wet and bedraggled.

He was straight-shouldered and rather stockily built. His dark straight hair dipped a bit over his high forehead. Soft brown eyes revealed his quiet manner. Standing there in his brother's tanning shop, he seemed almost short, measured against the pile of hides stacked high on the sorting table.

"We'll see, Mr. Baggy-pants," John said, meaningfully eyeing the work to be done.

"But, John, I can't wait. She needs her suitcase this afternoon. If I'm going, I'd better start now."

John laughed. Seating himself nonchalantly on the worktable, he leaned back against the hides and said, "Well, Dan, you've got a lot to learn about girls."

"I have?"

"Yes!" John Kress seemed to enjoy his young brother's frustration. He positioned one lanky leg over the other knee

and placed his hand on his ankle in a man-about-town stance
before he spoke. The warm July sun beamed through the open
window, shining full on John's black hair and his ample moustache, which almost obscured his pleasant smile. He decided
it was time for some brotherly advice.

"We fellows rush madly about to be on time," John went
on. "Then we wait, and we wait. Girls love to keep a fellow
waiting. Why, one time I sat in the parlor for ten minutes, maybe
more. The girl's little brother came in to visit with me. He told
me his sister had been all ready long before I got there. They
love to keep us waiting! You'll learn. Isn't Etta having a photograph made tomorrow?"

"Yes, in the morning. That's why she wants to get her valise
today. She's leaving in the afternoon."

"Take your time, little brother. She most likely will be washing her tresses when you arrive, or pressing yards and yards of
ruffles, or whatever else girls do in their spare time."

"John, tell me something."

"Yes, Dan?"

"Should I—should I lead out in the conversation, or should
I let her take the lead?"

"I'd say you take the lead. You're the man." John slapped
Dan warmly on the shoulder. "Aren't you the fellow who
coasted downhill with your eyes shut? Aren't you the fearless
one who played duck on the rock until you got your teeth
knocked out? Don't worry, you'll make out all right with the
girls, Dan. Just be debonair. How is it that father says it in
German—*anständig?* You know, the gentleman. She's a nice
girl, and smart, too. Here's my blessing." John shook Dan's
reluctant hand.

"I don't really need your blessing. Just tell father where I
am, will you?"

"Father!" John jumped to the floor. Brushing the dust from

the seat of his pants, he said firmly, "I'd better get back to work. So long, Dan."

There were two surprises in store for Daniel when he arrived at Chippewa Hill, Ontario, later that afternoon.

He found the keen-eyed Lauretta Eby neither washing her long brown hair nor waiting idly behind closed doors to make a dramatic appearance. With all her dainty 103 pounds, she was dressed and waiting on her aunt's front porch.

Expecting to see John instead of Dan as her chauffeur, Etta was also in for a pleasant surprise. Was not this the "Mr. Seventeen" she had wanted to meet? Her cheeks were pleasantly pink as Dan helped her into the high seat of the phaeton.

"Thank you, Dan. Looks as if someone has shined up the surrey," she observed. "It looks nice." She straightened her full skirt and settled herself comfortably in the far end of the long seat. "It's good of you to take time out from your work just for me, Dan."

Dan was somewhat abashed. What was it John said? "Be debonair—*anständig*."

"My pleasure." He smiled, then could think of nothing else to say, except "Get up, Prince," as he slapped the sleek horse on the back with the reins.

Lauretta took over the conversation. "I've had such a good time here this vacation. I hate to leave. You weren't out at the party at the lake last night. We had so much fun. The sunset was perfect on the water. We all stayed out in the boat until nine o'clock. So you are the bookkeeper in your family's tannery? Do you like the work?"

"Yes, I like it." Dan was getting tongue-tied again. Why didn't the words come when he needed them? "It's a nice day, isn't it?" he managed.

"Yes, and I'm glad. What do we do in an open surrey like this when it rains?"

Dan laughed. "We'd hurry home, I guess."

"Did you hear about my cousin who's going to take my photo tomorrow? I'm glad I know the photographer. It will be easier that way. It's the first picture I will have ever had made." Lauretta giggled.

"Yes?" Dan was having a hard time.

Lauretta tried to think of something else to say. "Shall we talk about school?" she asked.

"I was to ask that question," Dan thought anxiously. Quickly he said, "Sure. Do you like school?"

That did it.

"I love school. I had the best time this year. They let me help in the library. I actually earned money. It seemed like a fortune to me—a hundred and fifty dollars! I bought the folks a new sofa for one thing—and we needed it—and a marble-topped table. Then I bought a new silk dress for myself." She hurried to explain, "It's the first one I ever had in my life. The rest of the money I put in the bank." Stopping for breath Lauretta added, "It's good to save money, isn't it?"

Dan laughed. "I guess so. I never could." Then he froze again.

Etta, searching for new items of interest, found many. She babbled on about everything in the earth, sea, and sky.

Debonair Daniel could think of very little, except "Yes," "No," or "Get up, Prince."

Upon reaching Aunt Sarah's place, they found the family getting ready for supper.

"Of course you'll stay," jolly Aunt Sarah coaxed, persuading the young couple. "We're having soup with hot biscuits and honey, and there's plenty for everyone."

Dan looked at Etta.

"Sounds wonderful," she said.

"What red-blooded man could refuse a supper like that?"

Dan asked, assisting Lauretta from the phaeton. "I'm—I'm—I'm afraid I wasn't very good company, Etta," he stammered. "Would you answer if—if I wrote to you?"

"Oh, sure."

"Maybe I will be better behind a pen." Dan chuckled a little awkwardly, pushing a wayward strand of dark hair out of his eyes.

Lauretta flashed a warm smile of encouragement. "Thanks for the ride. We should go in for supper now," she whispered.

Watching her walk out of sight as he tied Prince to the hitching post, Dan's courage hit a new low.

"I'm not much of a match for her," he thought, "but if she'll have me, she's the girl for me!"

He might have been even more utterly discouraged if he could have read her thoughts as she freshened herself for supper. Looking into the mirror, Etta Eby wondered, "How can a boy like that ever get acquainted with any girl?"

Now Where Is That
Buttonhook?

*T*HERE WAS nothing fancy about the schoolhouse. It was as ordinary as the old pump over the well. It housed eight grades, spelling bees, a potbellied stove, a recitation bench, slates and slate pencils, high-topped button shoes, pigtails, and teen-age pompadours.

What if the room was too hot by the stove and too cold by the windows? The children were warmed by the fire of love that saturated the room. They were kindled into action by their teacher's sparkling eyes and gentle commands. They were set aflame by her desire to light a candle in each heart that would burn a lifetime.

Miss Lauretta Eby must have had eyes in the back of her head, or was it her ears that were supersensitive? Quickly this tiny, personable, very young lady turned from her desk. Her sharp eyes, like those of a predatory hawk, caught a quick move in the seventh-grade row. Could that be Burt starting trouble again?

Walking quietly down the aisle to the corner of the room, Miss Eby stood straight and tall. Stretching to all of the five feet two inches she had been endowed with and balancing her miniature body on her tiptoes, she sized up the situation like a veteran from Scotland Yard.

She concluded that Burt was too busy studying. His long legs were stretched out to the middle of the aisle. Little Dolly,

13

the blonde fourth grader who sat across from Burt, was hiding her face behind her big geography book. She was crying. Suddenly Miss Eby noticed that Dolly's left shoe on Burt's side was unbuttoned from top to bottom.

Slowly she walked toward Dolly. Gently she whispered in her ear, "Dolly?"

"Yes, ma'am." Blue eyes brimming with tears looked up.

"Will you go to the cloakroom, please?"

Dolly obeyed.

Miss Eby turned to Burt. His face looked like a thundercloud. "On my desk, Burt, there is a red pencilbox. You will find a buttonhook in there. Please get it and bring it to the cloakroom for me."

"Yes'm." Burt obeyed, stomping noisily to the desk. When the door was closed behind them in the cloakroom, the teacher laughed. Her gray eyes sparkled.

"Well, you've had your fun, Burt. Suppose you be the gentleman now, and button Dolly's shoe for her, please."

"Yes'm."

They waited until he had finished.

"Now thank the gentleman, Dolly, and dry your tears. You may take your seat."

Dolly smiled and obeyed.

Miss Eby closed the door and looked Burt straight in the eye. "Burt, I taught school all last year. I didn't have one bit of trouble. Now I'd hate to break my record. You are one of my biggest boys. Why, you're taller than I am. I need your help."

"Aw, she's a bawl baby," Burt explained smartly.

"But you are the gentleman!"

"What's that?"

Miss Eby knew she had made her point. "You may take your seat, Burt. Thank you!"

That night, alone in her room, Lauretta wrote a letter. It

was good to have a pen pal to correspond with. Besides, Daniel Kress *was* better behind the pen than he was at spontaneous conversation.

There was pride and precision in the neat, easy-flowing handwriting of this methodical, meticulous little teacher. Her letters, like her personality, were fresh and interesting. Her interest in people was half of her charm. There was a quick keenness, a liveliness, a verve, that was inspiring to everyone, and especially to the opposite forces within Daniel Kress, the silent one who admired from a distance this sparkling bit of animation.

She wrote, "You asked how a teacher as small as I can manage these big eighth-grade boys. That is my problem at the present. I have one now I am concerned about. So far, so good, but I feel as if I am sitting on a keg of dynamite that might go off with the least provocation. Confidentially, I think he is working his way into a climax. I will keep you informed.

"We like it here in Buchanan, Michigan. My father is working at the Studebaker plant in town. It's a friendly town, with several industries, one railroad, and some nice stores and churches.

"I didn't tell you, Dan, that we have started going to the First-Day Adventist church. There is a large group of young people and always something going on. You know I like that. Right now we have a special project coming up between Thanksgiving and the Christmas holidays, that is, if the weather will accommodate us. Do you ice-skate? That sounds like a stupid question to ask any Canadian, but I never heard you say. I'm very fond of skating. One time I thought I was pretty smart to be able to jump a good-sized log, so I did it several times. I lost my caution, gained too much speed, and overshot my mark. I cleared the log all right, but went full speed over the dam and plummeted into the icy water. It was nearly my last skate, for

I went down under the water twice before I was rescued. Believe me, I still dread the water. So I'll try to stay on top of the ice this winter. Oh, I started to tell you about our project.

"We are having an ice carnival—with real prizes. Our pastor's son, Allen (my age), and I are planning a duo. He is a good skater, and I'm sure it will mean much practice for me to keep up with him. I try to go for practice each day after school. It's refreshing after a day in that hot schoolroom. I forget my worries and skate till suppertime. I love the clean fresh air, the sweep of the cold wind against my cheeks, the tingle of exhilaration.

"Your letters are too far apart. I'm also anxious to hear how your mother is. Please tell me about her illness. Write often.

"As ever your friend,
"Lauretta"

Maybe the day was gloomy and depressing. Wintry days are often dull and drab in Michigan. The schoolroom seemed noisy and restless. But that did not excuse Burt for purposely tripping Tommy by suddenly sticking his foot out into the aisle in front of him.

That Tommy hurt his face when he bumped against the desk as he fell seemed of little concern to Burt, the bully.

Grinning broadly, he growled, "Why can't you watch where you walk?"

Miss Eby stiffened to a tall five feet two inches. She gave a staccato command.

"The room may be excused for lunch. Burt, please keep your seat."

"Says who?" he muttered, and rose to leave.

The teacher was ready for this one. In one quick move she had Burt by the collar, and in one more move he was back in his seat. When the others had left, she talked sternly to him.

"I planned on you big boys to help with the little folks, not to hurt them, Burt," she began in a gentle motherly tone of voice. "You're going on thirteen years old. Before you know it, you'll be a man. I was think——"

"Aw, shut up!"

The words froze her like ice. Recovering, she went to the door. She called to an eighth-grade boy in the yard, then waited. In less than a minute she had her weapon, a firm maple switch. Before Burt knew what was happening, he was on the floor between the rows of seats and the maple switch was warming the seat of his pants. There were no halfway measures used by this teacher.

Burt begged for mercy. "Please, Miss Eby; I'll behave."

Miss Eby was out of breath. She trembled inwardly like a man with the shakes. But not a sign of her emotions showed through her brave camouflage.

"All right. Is that enough?" She got in an extra strike before Burt could answer.

"Yes, please."

"You may stay in your seat during the lunch hour. I'll bring your lunch pail to you. When you have eaten, you may write a note to your mother. Let me read it when you have finished. Is that clear?"

"Yes, ma'am."

"I'll go home with you after school. I'm here to help you, Burt—even if it takes a maple switch to do it."

If all mothers were more like Burt's mother, there would be fewer problem pupils. As she opened the door of her house to the teacher, she opened her own heart to help the teacher solve their mutual problem.

Weeks later in a hurried note to Daniel, Lauretta wrote:

"I no sooner get Burt settled than I wonder about you, Dan. But first I must tell you about my model pupil these days. And I don't mean Allen, the pastor's son, no matter what you say.

2

I mean Burt, the braggart. What a small maple switch will do is marvelous! His whole attitude has changed. His grades are better. Every prize I offer he wins honestly. He locks the schoolhouse for me. He even carries my books home from school. I told you I thought I could win him, and I'm so glad I have.

"Our Sunday School youth group call themselves the Pearl Gatherers. A nice name. Now here is the real news. I have been baptized and have become a member of our little church here. I want to be a real Christian and help others to be. You never say anything about your church interests, Dan. Tell me, what are your thoughts about it? Let me know.

"Oh, I didn't tell you about the ice carnival. You should have been here. You would have felt that suddenly Hans Brinker had come alive. It was too exciting. I can still hear the skates clicking on the ice as we raced to the bonfire and back. Would I sound too proud to say we won? I have learned to know Allen better, too, and we were successful with our duo. Even if there had been no prizes, it would still have been worth the effort.

"To keep physically fit is important, too. We owe it to ourselves and to our Creator.

"I am sorry about your mother's illness, Dan. Write more often.

"Your friend always,
"Etta"

A letter to Lauretta by return mail brought news that would suddenly change the life of her friend Dan from a carefree boy to a man of the world.

"Port Elgin, Canada
"1880

"My dear Lauretta:

"Mother died last week. I can't believe it yet! Everything is changed. Father has gone to live at my brother Philip's place. He's taking it so hard. Sometimes I have thought of my father as a severe man. He can be when his rules are disobeyed. One rule he has held for all ten of us is that as long as we live at home we must be in the house by nine o'clock at night. He will not spare the rod if we disobey. We have always spoken German at home, and I can still hear his voice, firm and positive. He definitely ruled his household. He is a small man, short and wiry, but very muscular. I am apt to give you the idea he was unjust. He was not. He has a kind heart, that I know, for I have seen him weep when our neighbor's barn burned to the ground.

"Now I feel like a baby bird thrown out of the nest by a storm. I think I will go to Detroit or Chicago and find work, and see this big world around me.

"I can't believe this has happened to us. I feel stunned. My mother has meant a lot to me, Lauretta. I can close my eyes and hear her gentle voice. She was always gentle. I can never remember of her slapping or whipping me, as most mothers do, though I'm sure I needed it many times. But this was her way. She took me off in a room by ourselves. She talked to me, looking me straight in the eye. When she knew I understood, she knelt with me beside a chair and asked God to help me be a better boy. Who can say which way is best? I only know that I loved her and miss her so much.

"I've enjoyed writing to you. I wish you success with your teaching. About this pastor's son, Allen, and the ice-skating. I don't know just what to say. Maybe the less I say, the better.

"As ever your friend,
"Daniel"

"Launch Out Into the Deep"

*B*UTTONS were high fashion in 1880. There were pearl buttons, brass buttons, silver buttons, padded fat ones, pressed thin ones, round ones, square ones.

Everyone was button conscious. Rows of buttons decorated ladies' suits; tiny neatly spaced buttons marched down the fronts of the long trailing dresses, or popped out conspicuously as an eye-catching item on the back of a garment.

At any rate, young, broad-shouldered Daniel Kress decided to see the world around him. Before long he was in Chicago, working, of all places, in a button factory. Now how long could a button factory challenge a young man of Dan's caliber? For those were stirring times.

Henry Ford, the same age as young Daniel, was working on his horseless carriage that would in a few years change Detroit into a mechanical melting pot.

Alexander Graham Bell had already made his famous speech by wire to his helper, Thomas A. Watson; and Luther Burbank had developed his wonder-working everbearing strawberry and the white blackberry. He had even made a cactus without thorns. "If the population of our globe should double," Burbank declared, "the world still could have enough food. We could live from the cattle and their by-products, and the cattle could be fed entirely on the spineless cactus grown on the Western plains."

"Go west, young man, go west" was the slogan of the day. Teddy Roosevelt, a victim of asthma, had gone west to try his luck with a rifle and a herd of buffalo.

Those were stirring times, restless times, thrilling try-it-yourself times. Daniel Hartman Kress did not stay long in the button factory!

When the circus with its gaudy glitter came marching up the Chicago streets, Dan's decision was immediate. What a marvelous chance to see the world! Enthusiastically he applied for a job, and he got it! He was not to feed the fat lady, or tease the tigers, or even to water the floppy-eared elephants; he was assigned the job of drawing the curtains for the horses and their riders to enter the ring!

Life for Dan was a dizzy merry-go-round of excitement.

"Be sure your instrument is well tuned before you play it," is a sensible adage. But Dan, like any boy in any age, had to take his own time "tuning up." He was a definite amateur. That the music his life could make might be uplifting or even sublime seldom entered his young mind. He walked into strange, dim places with an air of adventure. He heard strange music. Sometimes it thrilled him; sometimes it bored him; sometimes he hated himself, for often in the midst of an allurement a thought would appear that was as foreign to the atmosphere as a baby in an old folks' home. For an instant the music of a hymn surrounded him. Again Dan could almost hear his mother's gentle voice humming a once-familiar tune. Like a fresh breeze in the stuffy room, it gave momentary relief until the imaginary window suddenly slammed shut.

"Come on, fellows," he would call. "This one's on me." And another wasted hour slipped slowly into eternity.

During those next two years heaven looked down with pity on this daring Dan, who tried so desperately to see the world and become a part of it.

His evenings were usually spent in the hotel billiard rooms. It was the custom those days for fellows to congregate together in hotels and spend the evening at different games. He was one of the drinking, smoking, card-playing gang. Little was thought of indulging in a few drinks. One set up the first round, and another would add his share.

Dan's pockets were full of holes. At this rate it was hard to break even—let alone save money. Thinking to better his financial prospects, Dan accepted a job as bartender. All he needed now was a big black moustache to complete the picture! The picture might be comical if it hadn't been so tragic. But gradually, surely, Dan was learning that "life is a chalice to be filled —not a cup to be drained."

"Once to Every Man
and Nation"

*T*HE IMMENSE metropolis of Detroit, Michigan, which was once the state capital, today leads the world in the production of motor vehicles. How well its populace advertises its own products!

The four-lane superhighway, circling around Henry Ford's 1,050-bed hospital, is like a racetrack of wild horses. Each slick model is manned by an ever-alert jockey, with reins held firmly in his grip. At the red-light signal four lanes of shining steeds paw the earth and snort their disapproval. Tensely they wait. The light turns green! The stampede begins. It is a furious, fantastic race.

Touring Detroit today may be a unique thrill, but it was the bustling business of yesterday's carriage trade which made the change from carriages to cars so smoothly possible. Wagons, surreys, phaetons, buggies of every category, were the mode of travel in 1880. The hitching posts and the drinking troughs were a part of the city street's ordinary equipment.

If you walk along the apartment-lined streets of any big city today and study the faces of its people, you discover that many of them look anxious and hurried. Some look bored; some look burdened—yesterday was like today. Others, like Lauretta Eby, new in a large city, are plainly homesick and lonely.

Lauretta had taken a chance for advancement. She moved to Detroit and became the billing clerk for Frederick Stearns and Company, manufacturing pharmacists in the city. She boarded with a family friend. Lauretta found her work interesting, but she missed the church young people and her small-town friends. Her evenings were nearly always occupied with sewing or letter writing.

"Lauretta," a voice called from the hall. There was a knock on her door.

"Yes, Mrs. Gordon?" She opened the door. "Come in. I've just finished writing a letter to my folks."

"Oh, fine. Tell them hello for me." Mrs. Gordon took a seat as she spoke. She was a tall, spindly person, neat and pleasant.

As she folded the letter, Lauretta commented, "They say no news is good news, but I still wish the folks would write more often."

"Well, I have some news for you." The landlady's smile was genuine. "And it's good news, too. Better sit down, Etta." She laughed.

"There's a handsome dark-haired gentleman waiting for you in my parlor this very minute!" Mrs. Gordon's intonation did justice to the news she carried.

"For me? In your parlor?" Etta looked surprised and then joyful. "Who is he? Tell me quick!" She grabbed her friend's arm insistently.

"He didn't say. But he has a handsome black moustache, and I'd judge he is about your age or a little older. Now hurry." Mrs. Gordon seemed excited too, and why not?

"Tell him I'm sorry to keep him waiting. I won't be too long."

Lauretta moved quickly as Mrs. Gordon left. She scanned her reflection in the long mirror. "Now look at me!" she worried. "He *would* come when I look my worst. My hair's a sight. What shall I wear?"

Holding the kerosene lamp in her hand, she searched her closet. "Why, I'll wear the very best dress I have," she decided, "the blue one with the lace on the collar."

Setting the lamp back on the stand, she kept right on talking to herself. "Now, Daniel, you can just wait. It's been two whole years since I have heard a word from you. By now—let's see— you were eighteen when your mother died. Hm-m-m-m-m—so you'd be nearly twenty-one. Well, well!"

The dressing process completed, Etta gave her reflection a last once-over in the mirror. Pinching her cheeks to make them pink, splashing a few drops of perfume on her best handkerchief, she walked regally down the open stairs into the parlor.

A little expectant, a little nervous, Lauretta held out her hand as the tall man rose from the horsehair sofa to meet her.

"Dan!" she exclaimed, totally surprised. "You—you look so —so different—you've—I can't believe my eyes!"

The debonair gentleman seemed pleased. "Do you like what you see?" he questioned, looking straight into her eyes; and before she could answer, he laughingly said, "I do."

Lauretta was somewhat flustered. "Why—yes, but——"

"Well, let me ease your mind. I'm not Dan. I'm John. You remember me, too, I hope?"

"Of course, John. Well, after all, it's been more than two years since I have seen either of you. Now where is Dan?"

"Dan? Oh, Dan got sick. Went back to Canada. But why don't we sit down, Etta? You're probably tired after a day in the office. I hear you've been promoted."

"Oh, yes. The bookkeeper got sick, so now I am doing the bookkeeping, too. It's a little different from teaching."

"I'll always think of you as a schoolmarm." John toyed nervously with his hat, then laid it down beside him. "Dan told me about your Bully Boy Burt, and how you got him to eat out of your hand."

"Well, that isn't exactly right. He didn't eat out of my hand, nor was he spoon-fed!" Etta laughed. "He earned everything he got, and he worked hard for it. I was very proud of him."

John eyed her curiously. "Say, how is the ice skater?"

Lauretta blushed a bit. "Why does he ask so many questions?" she wondered.

"Ice skater? Oh, that! I haven't been ice-skating since I came to Detroit. Aren't the Canadians the ice skaters? I thought you boys would all be famous hockey players."

"Hockey is Canada's game all right, but we Kresses never got started on it. There's always a living to make at the tanning shop, you know; and we have spent most of our time working. But didn't you have an ice-skating partner in Buchanan, Etta?"

Lauretta walked mentally around that pointed question and decided to avoid it as if it were a viper. She stepped into a field of thought entirely new. "You said Dan was sick, John. I hope it's nothing serious."

"Well, no. I think he was more homesick than anything else. Things have been different since mother died, you know. It seems Dan is the worse for it. He's been restless and unsettled. You remember the old family rule, 'In the house by nine o'clock'? Dan has gone all out to prove to himself and the rest of us that rules don't count. He's a night owl, and he worries me. Frankly, Lauretta, he needs a good girl to help him find himself and get his feet on something solid. If he wrote you again, would you answer him?"

Etta smoothed the lace on her dress with graceful fingers before she answered. "Why, yes, John; I'd answer him. I've always answered his letters promptly."

John smiled as he picked up his black hat. Rising to his feet, he walked slowly to Lauretta's chair. "Dan's always been a little special to me, Etta. I guess you know that. I feel even more concerned about him since mother died. I'll tell him I saw you."

"Thanks, John. I'm glad you came, even if I did mistake you for Dan. Forgive me, won't you?"

Walking slowly up the stairs after John had left, Etta began to cry. If she had known then what later she learned, she would have foregone the tears, for the said Daniel Hartman Kress was not in Canada at all. He was waiting timorously around the corner for John. And John was instantaneously bombarded with anxious questions:

"What does she look like, John?"

"Will she write to me?"

"What about that minister's son?"

"Was she mad because I hadn't written?"

"Do you think she cares anything for me?"

"What would you do, John?"

All this and more. After much discussion as they walked along, John gazed intently at Dan. "Dan, I'm going to be brutally frank with you. Etta looked beautiful. She walked down those stairs like a queen. She had on a blue dress with a lace collar. She may not be as pretty as some girls, but she is beautiful in a different way. She has a queenly way about the way she holds her head, the way she walks, as if she knows what life is all about and wants to be a part of things that will go somewhere. She's smart, and she's a lady. You want my idea? I think you'd be a fool to let any parson's son get ahead of you. Why don't you straighten out your life and show her you can be worthy of her? She'd make a fine wife for you. Believe me, if you don't, there are other fellows who will!"

Dan swallowed hard and blinked his eyes. Somehow he didn't feel like talking anymore. They walked on in silence— silence that was warm and companionable, silence that was sound and solid. This was silence of love more meaningful than words. A loving Creator looking over Dan's shoulder must have been happy to see the influence of John's words.

Later that week Daniel penned this letter to a certain girl in an "Alice-blue gown":

"Dear Lauretta:

"I feel as though I owe you an apology. The past two years of my life have been more than wasted. I'm ashamed to say they have been spent in a fruitless search to see the world and copy its ways of life.

"I want to beg your forgiveness for neglecting your friendship. I really have always cared for you, although I have never said so. I would be bold to ask again for your affections. I promise you I will write more faithfully and try to prove myself worthy of your friendship. Please answer my letters.

"John sends his warmest regards.

"Your true friend,
"Dan"

Prompt as usual, the answer came in the familiar feminine handwriting.

"Daniel, my Friend:

"Thank you for your kind letter. I am sorry to hear that you were sick and went home to Canada. By now you should be feeling better. At least you didn't mention it, and that should be a good sign. Of course, by now you know that John was here to see me. At first I thought it was you with the black moustache. I was somewhat disappointed to find it was John instead, for I wanted to see you and talk to you. But it was kind of him to stop by.

"I have always valued your friendship, Dan. I've missed your letters these past two years, and felt neglected and hurt, too. Can you blame me?

"Of course you're trying to find yourself. So am I, Dan. As John said to me, 'I think of you as a schoolteacher, and now here you are a bookkeeper.' I *am* finding myself, and if I can use all these things I learn to make a better life in the future, it will be worth it. So will yours.

"You say you are not worthy of my affections. I feel as though I haven't really known you yet. It wouldn't be fair to say I did care for you or didn't care for you, because I haven't known you well enough to say. I do welcome your friendship and hope to know you better. Love and marriage are far too sacred to be taken lightly. I want no regrets afterward.

"Detroit is a big city, and I do get lonely. Your letters are always a welcome treat. It's good to see that familiar handwriting on the envelope again. Now that we are pen pals once more, write often. I like it.

"Affectionately,
"Lauretta"

"1884 New Year's Day

"My dear Etta:

"How strange it seems to write 1884! What better way to start a new year than to write to you? Besides, I have something very important to tell you that can't wait.

"Last night was the big night, of course. As usual, I was at the hotel billiard room. It has by now become like home because that old gang of mine has really made a habit of it. The usual group was there last night, as well as a group of strangers who joined us at cards and games.

"One gets to know his own group pretty well after two years. There are the faithful ones who stay by you when you've had one drink more than they have; there are the spongers who depend on the generosity of others; there are the slaphappy ones who can't afford to treat and can't resist either. There are the jolly life-of-the-party ones, and some who are ready to pick a fight after a few drinks. One gets used to the setting—the smoky, overheated rooms, the noise, the laughter, and the moods.

"Last night's activities I must tell you about. I shall never forget it. The first part of the evening was ordinary, except for the visitors and the festive atmosphere. We all drank, we smoked, and we played games.

"At midnight we gathered around the bar, our glasses filled with whiskey. Suddenly one of our group shouted, 'Let's all swear off!'

"We all clashed our glasses together and took what was supposed to be our last drink.

"With all my heart I meant it, and I still do. But before the evening was over, some of the boys had indulged again. We played later than usual. As I watched the others, something very strange happened to me. I began to think (a thing I have done too little of lately). I cannot help believing that my mother's prayers for me were being answered and that the seeds she had planted in my heart when I was small suddenly began to come to life. I could almost hear her gentle prayers as we used to kneel by the chair in the kitchen.

"Then, Lauretta, in the flickering glow of the kerosene lamps, all at once things looked strange to me. I saw my friend Tom so drunk he couldn't walk home. I had seen him that way before, but now I thought about his wife and how she would feel seeing him in this condition. I thought about his children and their reaction to him. Why hadn't I thought of these things before?

"Then there was old Marty. He was slumped over the table, blubbering and slobbering and ready to fight. There were Frank and Bill—how could they find their way home alone? Then I saw some visitors. Two hours before, they came into the hotel, beautifully dressed women and snappy, well-groomed men, all out for a big time. Now they were silly, slobbering, loud-mouthed humans ready to accept any invitation to any evil suggestion.

"All at once I hated it. The whole thing was repulsive to me.

The air was heavy, and so was my heart. With God's help, Lauretta, I'll never touch another drop. I want to be a decent man. I've seen all kinds these two years. Now God has forgiven me. I hope you will, too.

"This year should mean something special in our lives. I want to prove myself to be a man you can admire. I want to be worthy of your love.

"Sincerely your friend,
"Daniel

"P.S. The New Year's bells are silent now. The first day of the year of 1884 is crispy white and frosty cold. But I have found a new warmth of courage. Perhaps this year, of all the years of our lives, will be the best so far. A very happy New Year to you, Lauretta. Let's write often. Dan."

Tears and Trousseau

*A*PRIL WALKS into Michigan like a flower girl at a wedding. No wedding would be complete without a flower girl. She is frequently the main attraction, and she knows it. She makes the children laugh; the middle-aged forget their worries, and the old folks smile proudly. Walking down the aisle, this little midget can keep in perfect step, but she seldom does. She delights in doing the most unexpected things. She may forget to drop her perfumed petals on the bridal path and suddenly decide to shower grandpa and grandma instead.

Whimsical is the word for young Miss Spring. But who can blame this little lady for being a bit whimsical as she leads the parade into summer? She circles and spins, wheels and whirls, as she heads northward into Detroit and Canada.

One warm, languid afternoon, as April was mellowing into May, Lauretta finished her day's work. She walked slowly toward the big office door which read, "Frederick K. Stearns, Manager."

Timidly she knocked on the door.

"Come in."

"Mr. Stearns, I'd like to speak with you, please."

"Yes, Miss Eby?" Kind eyes looked up from the papers on the desk.

"I think I should tell you that I may be married this summer." Etta never was the kind to beat around the bush. "I thought you ought to know in time to get someone to take my place."

"Well, now, that will be a hard thing to do. You have been a faithful worker, and we appreciate your work."

"Thank you, sir. You know I've got two weeks' vacation coming. I was wondering if I could plan to leave by the middle of June. That'll give you time to get someone, and it would give me time to go home and get some sewing done."

"That sounds logical to me," Mr. Stearns agreed. "But I want to tell you something, Miss Eby. Our door is always open to you, just in case you want to give this young man his walking papers. You might decide you'd rather be an old maid!" His eyes twinkled as he shook her hand and said good night.

Her head in a happy whirl, the bride-to-be went on a shopping spree. Starry-eyed, she purchased lace and ribbon, thread and buttons, and yards of gorgeous fabrics for her trousseau.

With dreams for company she started the long walk home to her room. Giggling girls poured out of the shops at quitting time, joining the flood of people already hurrying in and out of the stores. Mature ladies modeling the latest fashions moved with make-believe comfort, trailing their long sweeping skirts through the town. Moustached men mingled on the street corners to discuss their mutual problems. Each face was interesting, Lauretta decided, for within each life was the same happiness, the same heartache, the same hope, which she carried in her own heart.

Walking out of the shopping area into the little streets lined with small homes, she slackened her pace. Picturing her own future, she almost envied the young mothers playing with their children in the small fenced-in backyards.

Questions filed through her mind in orderly fashion. What of my own future? Do I really love Daniel? Why am I sometimes so sure and sometimes so uncertain? Do other couples feel this way too? How can I really know him when our only contacts have been through letters? Was I fair to refuse to become engaged until after I see him and feel as though I know him better?

What about our religious differences? What about Dan's tobacco habit? the evenings at the hotel? Would he miss his way of life when we have our own home? What if I would yet lose him altogether? Then I'd really be alone.

Alone! Alone! The words kept step with her feet as Lauretta watched the sunset streak the sky. They worried at her heels as she walked along. Then a prayer reached long arms of faith to God, who could see the future. Thankful tears sparkled in the glow of the sunset.

*   *   *   *   *

The small town of Buchanan, Michigan, accepted its excited visitor without much ado. Bubbling with joy at being home, Lauretta opened her suitcase and took out a mysterious parcel. Laying it in her mother's lap, she said happily, "Look, Mother; this is for my wedding dress!"

"Wedding dress?"

"Yes, Mother; and I thought I'd use this material to make my undies."

"Undies?"

It was obviously a new word to Mrs. Eby. Etta ignored the surprise in her mother's voice.

"I thought I could make them up now, and when Dan comes —well, maybe I better explain, Mother. You know, Dan and I haven't seen much of each other, although we have kept the mailman busy. When Dan asked me to marry him, I told him I didn't feel I knew him well enough. He promised to come here the first of July, and we'll see more of him. So if I like him, fine; and if I don't—well, I can still use the clothes I'll make."

Mrs. Eby was a slim, straight-shouldered woman. She wore

her dark hair parted in the center and pulled back tightly to make a bun at the nape of her neck. She spoke hesitantly. "That sounds sensible, Etta. Much depends on the choice you make." Her kind gray eyes smiled approvingly at her daughter, but her face was serious. Turning toward Etta, she added almost as an afterthought, "Marriage lasts a lifetime, you know."

Lauretta bristled like a banty rooster. "I know, Mother! Why do you think I've put him off this long?"

"Laurie." Mrs. Eby seldom called her daughter that name. It had the desired effect. Etta's blood pressure suddenly dropped to normal. "Laurie," her mother went on as if planning each word, "does Dan ever show any interest in church affairs or anything religious?"

It was the one question of all questions which Lauretta had dreaded. She must face it head on. There was no way to avoid it.

"No, I can't say he has. But, Mother," she added hurriedly, "he is a fine man. He had a wonderful mother. She was a Christian woman, and he thinks all women should be like her."

Mrs. Eby seemed to ignore the pleading words of her daughter.

"Do you remember when you were first baptized in the little church here?" She waited for the answer.

"Why, yes, of course!"

"You had big dreams of being a missionary. China, wasn't it?" Mother's hands smoothed over the soft white material that lay like a kitten in her lap. "How can you carry out your dreams with a husband who's not even interested in the church? We want you to be happy and have a Christian home, like your father and I have had. Please pray about it, dear."

"Of course, Mother; I always do. Why are you trying to discourage me? I feel like—I feel like going back to Detroit to work." Dropping the parcel of ribbons and lace that she was going to show her mother, Etta started to leave the room.

"Laurie." There it was again. Mrs. Eby put her gentle hands on her daughter's shoulders. Looking tenderly into her tear-filled eyes, she said without a ruffle in her sweet voice, "Laurie, dear, you're precious to your father and me. We only want you to be happy. It's hard enough when both of you are working for the same things. You know what happens when a team of horses won't pull together. Could you right now drop your way of life and accept his way?" It was a pointed question.

Dropping her eyes to shut out her mother's penetrating gaze, Lauretta wondered how much of Dan's life her parents knew. She answered her mother's query plainly. "No, Mother, I guess not."

"Then be sure he will be willing to come your way in the future. It can't possibly work otherwise."

"But, Mother, you don't know Dan. He's making progress. When he decides to do a thing, he does it. He has proved that!"

Thinking of the New Year's resolution that he had kept, Etta wondered how much she should tell her mother. Should she tell anything at all? She longed to justify in her mother's sight the man she loved. What would mother think if she knew about his smoking and card playing and the night life he enjoyed?

"There is one thing you must know, Mother," she substituted. "Dan has high ideals. He believes in his mother's ways and in her prayers. He said so. Can't you see? It's all in the background. It—it just hasn't been answered yet. He has a better education than either Philip or John has, and they have both made good."

Mrs. Eby considered the problem thoughtfully. "You're right, Etta; and if you have faith in him, then we should, too. Tomorrow let's start cutting out the wedding dress. What do you say?"

Etta's face beamed. She hugged her mother impetuously.

"Mother," she said, "you are a darling! You'll never know how much this means to me." Planting a warm kiss on her mother's cheek, she declared, "I'm sure I'm the happiest girl in Buchanan, Michigan!"

In the two wonderful weeks that followed, the pale blue ribbon was inserted in its lacy background; the ruffles were properly edged with tiny lace; the hems were caught with the gossamer thread of bridal dreams; the buttons matched the handmade buttonholes, and the result began to look like a trousseau. The white wedding dress was a practical, neat creation with rows of tiny buttons marching meticulously down the back. There was still the hem to sew and the last finishing touches to add when, out of a blue sky, Lauretta got an idea. She decided her eyes needed a rest from sewing.

Walking past their small church on her way to the store, Etta decided to see if her pastor was in his study.

"Well, well. Here's one of our favorite Pearl Gatherers!" Pastor Farnum's warm hand welcomed her. "And how do you like the big city, young lady?"

"I really don't," Lauretta returned. "I think I'm going to make a change. Maybe you could help me, Pastor."

"Go on; go on. It sounds interesting. Do you have a call from China?"

"China? Oh, no, Pastor. I wanted to ask you if you would marry me?"

Pastor Farnum laughed heartily. "That's the best proposal I've had in forty years, and this isn't even leap year." Then sobering, he added, "Lauretta, there's nothing I'd rather do in the world than to marry a fine Christian couple. He is a Christian, of course?" There it was again, that unavoidable question.

"I wish with all my heart that he was. But so far he hasn't made that decision."

"What a shame! And you're the girl who would go to—

where was it—India, or China?" The pastor's glasses were suddenly raised above the bushy dark eyebrows to rest out of the way on his high shiny forehead.

Lauretta seemed a little annoyed. "But he *is* a good man, and I have a lot of faith in him. I want you to meet him, and you'll feel the same as I do. If you don't, I'll be surprised."

The pastor put out his warm, friendly hand. "I'll withhold any judgment. I'm sure you know him better than I, my young friend. Now just when will I meet this gentleman?"

"He plans to come the first of July," Etta answered as she left. "I'll bring him over to meet you, Pastor." Her smile was sincere and genuine. But why did the smile so suddenly disappear? Without realizing it, the young bride-to-be was nearly dragging her feet as she walked home. Her thoughts seemed to be chained to her ankles.

In spite of her doubts she was determined to follow the dictates of her heart and the leading hand of God. Her step quickened. The future may seem eternal and unknown, yet it begins one step at a time—one step at a time—one step at a time.

Little wonder Lauretta Eby was filled with mounting excitement, counting the last few days until Dan would arrive, not like a knight on a white steed with a popcorn bridle, but as a passenger on the Michigan Central Railroad.

Singing happily, Lauretta went to the station by herself that day, July 1. She was early, as usual. It felt good to rest a bit on the green bench in the waiting room, for the day had been hot and sultry.

"My hair!" Etta thought suddenly. "I better check it again." She rose nervously from the bench and hurried to the ladies' room. One does not meet a man like Dan just any day. Primping and preening before the mirror, she asked herself, "Should I kiss him when he gets off the train? How else can one know if she loves a person?" She blushed at the thought of such a wild idea. Walking slowly into the lobby, she stood before the unmoving clock.

The stationmaster came by. He smiled. "You're looking mighty pretty, Miss Eby," he remarked as he took a seat behind his desk.

"Oh, thank you, Mr. Dunlap. I'm expecting my fiancé!"

"Your fee-on-what?" He laughed as he pushed his glasses into place. "Now that's news for the paper." He glanced at the schedule. "Yes, ma'am. There's the whistle now. One more minute, and you'll be in his arms." He chuckled as he made his way to the platform.

Why do train whistles accelerate the heartbeat? Scanning each approaching face with eager anticipation, Lauretta stood on her tiptoes. She walked closer. She looked anxious.

The conductor, helping an old lady alight from the high step, cautioned, "Careful now; there's no hurry."

"That's all," he announced, waving his long arms. "All aboard!" Then to Lauretta he added, "You enter by the front car, young lady."

"No, sir, I'm not a passenger. I am—I was looking for someone—that is—are you sure?—there must be someone else in that train." Etta's unbelieving voice betrayed her emotions.

"That's all. I'm sorry, young lady." Seeing her expression of utter disappointment, he added, "Better luck next time." Lifting the portable step, he closed the heavy door with a bang.

"The Law of the Medes
and Persians"

J WILL positively not go down to meet another train!" When Lauretta Eby made this decision, she meant it. She had not only met one train and been utterly disappointed, but several. To be teased by her parents was bad enough, but to be laughed at by Mr. Dunlap, the stationmaster, was even worse. She would shed no more tears. Enough was plainly enough!

Mrs. Eby hung the wedding dress carefully out of sight. Why rub salt in an open wound? Besides, there were other things to sew which were not so poignantly connected with the affairs of the heart.

Etta put on the bravado act. She was gay and overly talkative. Laughing brightly, she said, "I may have my faults, Mother, but being wrong is not one of them!"

A twinkle sparkled in mother's eyes. "We've been afraid of that. From the time you were a tiny thing, you were the I'll-show-them-I-can-do-it kind. When you were younger, we had a frisky horse named Blondy. Your father told you never to touch her, but one snowy winter day you harnessed that horse, hitched her to the cutter, and away you went. Blondy knew there was a new driver behind her, and she ran as fast as she could for two miles. There was a fine of five dollars for crossing a certain bridge too fast, but so what? You drove her a mile farther before you could stop her. When you went into your father's shop later, he was dumbfounded.

43

" 'Does your mother know you are here?' he asked.

" 'No,' you answered.

" 'How did you hitch Blondy to the cutter?'

" 'Just like you do, Daddy.'

"To help you see the folly of your choice, father put the reins in your hands and took the whip to Blondy. He said you hung on for dear life, and once you were home, your arms ached for hours. You had learned your lesson on that one. You never tried it again!"

"That's the way I learn best," Etta sighed. "Maybe this is the same kind of lesson."

A loud knock rattled the front door. Dropping her sewing in the chair, Lauretta hurried to answer it. A tall, skinny boy holding a yellow envelope stood on the front porch.

"Are you Lauretta Eby?" he asked.

"Yes."

"Telegram for you. Just sign here, please."

Lauretta's eyes reflected a million questions as she scribbled her name hastily on the pad. Eagerly taking her telegram, she closed the door and ran upstairs to her room.

"Mother! Mother!" Like a flash Etta ran right back down the stairs again. "It's from Dan, Mother. He'll be on the 7:15 tonight!" Etta's eyes glowed with happiness.

Her mother's eyes sparkled right back. "But what about your 'law of the Medes and Persians,' Etta?" she said, laughing. "I thought you were going to stop meeting trains."

Throwing both of her arms impulsively around her mother, she answered, "Only love can revoke 'the law of the Medes and Persians.' I do hereby set my seal of approval on this revocation!" Kissing her mother's cheek, she laughed delightedly.

"Lauretta"—Mrs. Eby seemed serious—"I do believe you love that man."

"Mother, I believe you're right!"

In the four hours which followed, "the law of the Medes and Persians" was completely ignored. As the pretty Eby girl walked to the Michigan Central Railroad station this time, she was accompanied by her tall smiling father. By his presence he seemed to say, "This is my daughter. I must be the first to see this man who seems to have such power over her. There must be something special about him." And there was.

There went that train whistle again!

Father smiled down at his daughter as she squeezed his hand.

Mr. Dunlap hurried by. A knowing look spread like a naughty child's teasing grin over his face.

"All things come to those who wait," he muttered as he hustled out of sight.

The big doors of the coach opened with a bang. The conductor put the portable step in place.

"There he is, Father!" Etta let go of her father's hand and stepped ahead expectantly.

Dan, handsome in his black hat and dark suit, set his valise down on the platform. It seemed the most natural thing in the world for him to take her in his arms and kiss her.

All the doubts of yesterday disappeared; all the desires of today pressed close; all the hopes of tomorrow waited impatiently for their attention.

Blushing happily, Etta announced proudly, "Father, this is my Daniel!"

"Good evening, sir. I'm glad to know you." There it was again—the warm, winsome smile of Daniel Kress.

The hand of the lover and the hand of the father met in a firm handclasp. Dan's warm brown eyes seemed to seal a bond of affection between the two most important men in the life of Lauretta Eby.

"You young folks must have much to say to each other, I

know, Dan," said father when supper was over. "The river road along the old Saint Joseph is the beauty spot of the country. Wouldn't you like to take the buggy out? The horses need a little exercise, you know. How about it, son?"

How much of the countryside they saw is debatable. After they returned, only one subject seemed to be important.

"We want to be married next Sunday, Mother, Father. Will that work out with you? Help us decide about the wedding, will you, Mother?" Etta's eyes reflected the happiness she felt. Sitting round the dining-room table, they laid their plans.

Before the day of the wedding Dan had won to his heart not only the bride, but the parents of the bride, the church pastor, and even the Pearl Gatherers. Who could resist his quiet way, his friendly understanding, his kind manner? There was very little brusqueness or bustle in the ways of this man. Was this why he seemed such a perfect mate for the brisk, positive, self-assured little lady he had chosen for a wife? Certainly all who knew them both could see that each was a complement for the other. Perhaps that is one reason why the parents were so easily persuaded.

At any rate, the Pearl Gatherers outdid themselves decorating the church for this particular wedding. An arch of pure white lilies framed in greenery made a beautiful background for the young lovers. The little church and even its pastor seemed proud to unite this pair in holy wedlock.

The gold-rimmed spectacles stayed long enough on the pastor's generous nose to read the scripture needed for the service. Then, as though their duty was done, they dangled in his hand as he gave a lengthy dissertation on marriage and its responsibilities. After adding his pastoral blessing, Pastor Farnum introduced the happy couple to their friends. Could the kindly pastor have looked ahead fifty years, he would have known that he had played a part in beginning a very happy marriage.

In their hotel room in Detroit that night, the new bride showed her husband an exquisite wedding gift. It was a Bible given to her by her special friends, the Pearl Gatherers. Slowly Lauretta turned its new pages admiringly.

"It's beautiful, isn't it, Dan? Look at the illustrations! Why don't we start our life together by making a habit of reading God's Word each day?"

"You do remind me of my mother, Etta. Go ahead and read."

Lauretta began: " 'I am the true vine, and my Father is the husbandman. . . . Abide in me, and I in you. As the branch cannot bear fruit of itself, except it abide in the vine . . .' "

Etta's voice was clear and pleasant to hear. Dan had lived in Michigan fruit country long enough to know that what she was reading from John 15 made good sense. When she had finished, he said, "Laurie, you pray. I haven't prayed since I was a little boy."

Together they knelt by the big chair, his warm arm about his precious girl who reminded him so much of his mother. That prayer meant a lot to both of them, even though it was not offered by the head of the family.

". . . and hand in hand help us to walk together with Thee, through whatever Thou dost have in store for our future. So help us, God, we ask in the name of Thy dear Son. Amen."

Daniel kissed his bride as they arose from their knees. There were tears glistening in his eyes as he held her in his arms. "God help me to be worthy of you, dear, and to make you always as happy as you are tonight."

Those words echoed down the corridor of days that stretched far into the future, the future that was to scoop this couple up in its grasp and settle them in a place of need that even now they could not imagine.

"I'm So Proud of You!"

*T*HE HONEYMOON wasn't over! In fact, it had hardly begun, for Etta and Dan were still in the busy metropolis of Detroit. Having a little time on their hands before the boat left the dock, they decided to call on Dan's old boss.

The old couple were delighted. "Imagine you young folk remembering us—and on your honeymoon besides. We feel honored, Dan."

Patting Dan's shoulder, the old German turned to his spry little wife. "Mother," he said happily, "how about a cool drink on a hot day? We could even have a toast to the beautiful bride —and the groom." Turning to Dan, he chuckled. "You noticed I didn't say beautiful groom?" His graying moustache nearly covered the jovial smile that made a wreath of happy wrinkles around his face.

"Come, come, let's go out on the porch. It's cooler there. I am so happy to meet your wife, Dan. I always said that a good wife is a man's best asset." Jostling the chairs to a comfortable position for everyone, he deposited his plump body in a sturdy rocking chair.

Hardly were they seated when Mrs. Goodendorst lowered a sparkling tray of refreshments in front of Etta. "On a hot day like this a cool drink should be just right, yes?"

"Oh, thank you; these cookies look good. You must be a fine cook, Mrs. Goodendorst."

4   49

"That she is!" her husband added quickly.

"Here—here is your drink, Etta girl." The hostess had the tall goblet of good German beer in her hand.

"Could I bother you for a glass of water instead, please? I—we—we don't use beer, thank you."

"Well, good for you! For that I fix you the best glass of lemonade you ever tasted. But—you, Dan, here." She held the goblet to Daniel.

"You could make mine lemonade too, please, Mrs. Goodendorst. You see, I swore off New Year's Day. I've seen so many fellows that couldn't stop on the first one."

"And so have I, Dan. I'm one of them right now. Make them all lemonade, Mother, please. Here, we should be a help to our young friends, and instead they are helping us."

On their way back to the hotel, Lauretta looked proudly at her new husband. His was a good face to look at for the rest of one's life, she decided. A feeling of warmth spread over her.

"Dan, I want you to know I was very proud of you tonight." Squeezing his arm, Lauretta clung to him. "Isn't it good to be working together for the same thing? I love you, Daniel Kress."

Dan patted her hand. "I hope it'll always be like this, sweetheart. A man's wife is his best asset."

*   *   *   *   *

A stiff breeze swept across the deck of the boat as it steamed upriver from Detroit, Michigan, to Southampton, Canada. The wind buffeted the hungry sea gulls that whirled and wheeled gracefully about the boat. They put on a real aerial ballet for the newlyweds. To the Kresses there were only two people who watched those gulls. To laugh, to talk, to make big plans for a happy future, to find a new togetherness in all their ventures— what more can a honeymoon mean?

When they arrived at Southampton, Dan and Etta were welcomed into Dan's brother's home until they could find a place of their own. They found a whole yardful of people waiting for them. Port Elgin boasted a fine band, and in true Canadian fashion they believed in welcoming their people properly. To the tunes of "Drink to Me Only With Thine Eyes," and "Darling Nelly Gray," and many others popular in 1884, the newlyweds were serenaded.

Baton in hand, the jolly band director beamed as they finished their first number. "Folks, Michigan is a wonderful place to find a good wife," he commented. "See for yourself, fellows. Our friend Dan, here, just took a ride on the Michigan Central Railroad to Buchanan, Michigan, and here she is! I want you all to meet the newlyweds, Daniel and Lauretta Kress."

The band struck up a new tune, the Kresses smiled their prettiest, and the front yard overflowed with fun and laughter as the refreshments were served.

"I have cookies, cakes, sandwiches, and cracknels. You folk help yourselves now." A pretty waitress stopped to serve them.

"Mary, you must have some good cooks around here," Dan remarked.

"We surely do," she replied. "Here, we forgot about your drinks!" and she turned to hand them each a full glass of good cold beer.

"Thank you, Mary, but if you don't mind, we'd rather have a glass of cold water."

"Oh, now, sure—just a minute." Mary seemed a little puzzled as she left, pushing her way through the crowd to the kitchen.

A new refreshment girl, seeing the bride and groom without any drinks, was much concerned. She shouted above the band music, "Why, you folks have no drinks! You were supposed to be served first. May I serve you?" Smiling graciously, she handed over two more glasses.

"No, thank you, Clara. Mary went to get us water. I—we've sworn off the other drinks."

Suddenly the band stopped as Clara shouted, "Sworn off? What's that?"

A kind friend, hearing the conversation, came to the rescue. "My dear girl, that simply means that Dan and Etta are smart enough to leave anything with alcohol alone. Now hurry out to the kitchen and tell the ladies to make two of the best glasses of lemonade they ever made in their lives for the bride and the groom. Here, Clara, I'll take that tray for you."

Again Lauretta looked up into the face of her husband. Again she reiterated her words, but this time they were silent. Only a look and a smile passed between them as the glasses of cold lemonade were placed in their hands.

*   *   *   *   *

Daniel was an avid baseball player. His enthusiasm for the game dated back to his high school days. Proudly he wore the title of captain of the Port Elgin team.

Standing before his bride at dinner-time, Dan smiled his most disarming smile. Proudly he announced, "We have a game coming up on Tuesday at Southampton, dear. Want to go along?"

"I'd love to, but——"

"But what?"

"But I'd be the only woman there, wouldn't I?"

"Well, I guess you would."

"In that case, I'd better stay here. I can visit with your sister. Maybe I could get the kitchen curtains made and fix up this place a little bit. When—when will you be back, Dan?"

"I'd say about ten or so."

"Ten o'clock at night? You play in the afternoon, don't you?"

"Yes, but the fellows always make it a special—have supper

and—and—well, it's the only time they have for a get-together."

"Ten, then." Etta said it as if she were writing it down in her mind.

On the day of the game, Dan's bride looked anxious as he said good-bye. He stood there with his arms full of bats and mitts and catcher's equipment. Looking boyish and happy in his uniform, he bent to kiss his wife.

"Have a good game," she said with a smile.

"Surely wish you could go along. You—you look worried. Is there something wrong, Etta?"

"No, not much." Etta tossed her head as she spoke.

Dan took her chin in his hand. "There, that's no way to say good-bye, sweetheart," he teased. "We promised not to have any secrets from each other, didn't we? Come now, what's the trouble?"

"All right, then I'll say just what I was thinking. All the fellows after the game—after supper—well—then what do they do?"

"We all play billiards or cards—you know. Just sit around, smoke, and talk."

"And drink?"

"Of course, Etta; but I don't. They all know that. We have a jolly time together, like a bunch of brothers who haven't seen each other for a while. Honey, don't worry your pretty head one minute. I haven't touched the stuff since January—February, March, April, May, June, July, August—that's seven, almost eight, months, isn't it?"

Etta felt ashamed. "All right, Dan; you've made your point. Have a good time. See you at ten."

"About ten," he repeated. Kissing his wife affectionately, Dan left. Later in the afternoon Etta, curtains in hand, walked over to Mary's place. Answering her knock, Mary asked bluntly, "Where's Dan?"

"Dan? Why, he went to the ball game. They play at Southampton."

"O Etta, why did you let him go?"

"Why not?" Etta asked, getting her sewing ready to work on.

"Why not? Maybe you don't know. All those fellows drink, and Dan's doing so well now."

"Mary, Dan has good sense. Why, he hasn't touched a drop for months. That's pretty wonderful. We have to trust each other."

Mary didn't sound very convinced, however. "I hope we won't be sorry. Let's forget it and get to work on these curtains. Say, have you seen the new sewing machines? They're amazing. Let's look for them the next time we get to the city."

"Someday maybe we can each have one! Wouldn't that be something?"

The afternoon seemed to have wings, and before long it was suppertime. Etta went home early. Nibbling at supper by herself was no fun. She gazed anxiously out the window and longed to hear Dan's steps on the porch. Restlessly she walked about the house. Mary had put a fear into her thoughts that was hard to shake.

The evening seemed endless. Lauretta found little consolation in writing a letter to her mother. It only brought to her mind more vividly her mother's concern for Dan's future. Leaving the letter unfinished, Etta decided instead to have prayer and take a nap on the couch.

But sleep would not come. When was an evening ever so interminable? Long before ten the worried bride began listening for footsteps. She even fancied her husband might love her so much he would come home early just to surprise her. But when the clock in the hall struck eleven, she was fully convinced that Dan had forgotten he even had a wife.

Sitting by the window so that she could hear better, Lauretta tried to sew. Every few stitches she stopped, looked, and listened, but she heard only silence broken by the sounds of the crickets and the katydids. A tense fear seized the girl. Could Mary have been right? Might Dan have weakened and had a drink with the boys? What if he would undo all he had accomplished in these last few months? Eleven thirty. The clock in the hall sounded like a broken record. "Trust each other—trust each other—trust——"

"How can I stand it?" Lauretta asked herself.

When the clock struck twelve, she knew she couldn't stand it any longer. Quietly, so that she would not waken anyone in the house, Etta crept down the stairs. The front door squeaked as she went out onto the porch. A path led out from the house to the lake. A full moon made the lawn look like a fairyland. In the shadows of the trees Etta stood a long time, watching the silver path of the moon on the water. Its beauty seemed to mock her. Restless and miserable, and still listening keenly for a familiar step, she cried silently.

At last she heard the footsteps. What if it wasn't Dan? Half frightened, she hid behind a tree so that whoever it was couldn't see her until she was sure she wanted to see him. Then she saw his face. It was Dan.

"Dan—O Dan!" She ran like a homesick child to the shelter of his arms.

"Etta, sweetheart! What are you doing out here?"

"O Dan, I'm so glad you're all right! You are, aren't you?"

"Of course I'm all right!"

"I've prayed for you all day."

"God bless you, darling. But I promised you I wouldn't drink with the fellows. Remember?"

"I know you did. But I could just see all of them coaxing you, and then I'd say to myself, 'We must trust each other,' until even the clock was saying it with me, over and over."

"You poor girl! And I thought you were tucked in your bed, peacefully sleeping. You don't need to worry anymore. What would you say if an old married man had decided to stay at home with his wife after this?" Cuddling his wife in the curve of his arm, he led her to the house.

"I'd say it was the smartest thing an old married man ever did." Etta's face was happy as she looked up at him in the moonlight. "You're a real Daniel, and I'm proud of you."

"Tonight I was in a real lions' den. As I watched my friends taking one drink after another, I studied their reactions. 'These are my friends,' I said to myself, 'but how can I help them?' I had plenty of chances to drink. Both teams were astonished that I didn't. At least I have given them a good example. Again tonight I determined to fight this thing if it is the last thing I do!"

Lauretta's happiness knew no bounds. "Dan, please kiss me again—I'm so proud of you!"

Come Into My Kitchen

J'VE NEVER cooked a meal in my life before, Katie." The words came hesitantly from the quivering lips of the new bride. Sitting at the table in her sister-in-law's cozy kitchen, Etta looked the picture of despair.

"But has anyone ever tried any harder than I have? I'd like to know." Jumping nervously from her chair, Etta pleaded, "Kate, you've just got to help me. I'll teach you to sew if you'll help me learn to cook. Will you? I can't go on like this—it was awful!"

"What was awful?" Kate was definitely getting interested.

"I'm ashamed to tell you, Kate. Dan went back to the brush factory hungry. I just now left him a couple of sandwiches to hold him over until supper."

Trying to hide the tears in her eyes, the bride toyed with the lace on her dress. "I was never so let down in all my life."

"What happened, Lauretta? Come on, tell me!"

"Well, ever since we moved by ourselves I've cooked potatoes and beefsteak and beefsteak and potatoes. I didn't know how to cook anything else, and Dan was getting so tired of it. There was a lot of steak left over this morning, so I cut it up and decided to make a stew for a change. Then I noticed a small bag of sage leaves I had drying behind the stove. Mary gave them to me, and she said they were good to use in roasts, so I put a handful in the stew."

Kate interrupted anxiously. "A handful? O Etta, didn't you taste it?"

"No, I guess I didn't. I just went on my happy, ignorant way, glad to have something different. When Dan came home, I told him to hurry and wash because we had a very special dinner. Well, we sat down, he asked the blessing, and served our plates. He took a big spoonful and made an awful face! 'Tastes like soap!' he said. Was I surprised!

" 'Etta, what did you put in the stew?' he asked.

" 'How could it taste like soap?' I wondered. Then I tasted it, and it did taste exactly like soap!"

Kate's brown eyes twinkled with laughter. "It sounds like the story of the three bears," she said.

"It wasn't too funny, Kate. We couldn't even eat the stew. You've just got to help me, or poor Dan will starve!"

"You poor thing! It would be tragic if it weren't so funny! 'For better or for worse' is really true for you two, isn't it? Now you come on out into my kitchen. We're having good old vegetable soup and johnnycake for supper. I'll show you how to make some too, Etta. You can really shock him tonight."

That night was a night to remember.

Dan, still hungry from his noonday fast, opened the front door with a brave, determined look on his face.

"Am I starved!" he exclaimed. Then he took one sniff and froze like a statue. "Wait—a—minute—sweetheart! What do I smell?" Dan kissed his wife questioningly. "You had me worried this noon," he admitted. "But this looks like a party. I like the flowers on the table."

"Well, thank you, kind sir. Your supper is ready, and guess what? Kate is teaching me to cook."

"Good! I'm all for that. Before long I'll have a wife, a bookkeeper, a housekeeper, and a cook all in one. That's the life!"

Etta beamed happily. "Now all I need is to have him say the supper is good," she thought.

Quickly Lauretta tucked away her brand-new and very precious recipes. Gradually she would add to her interesting collection. Soups, salads, roasts, breads, desserts—all these were part of the challenge of the happy future. But for today it was quite enough to hear the sweet words, "That was a good supper, Etta."

Trying to be efficient managers of their household, the Kresses sat down together to evaluate their needs for the winter months ahead.

With pencil in hand they plotted their course. Dan made the first suggestion. "Wouldn't ten bushels of potatoes be about right? That would be two bushels a month for—say five months." So they stored in their cellar for the winter ten bushels of potatoes, two bushels of onions, and two dozen cabbages. Months later they were to learn that half as much would have been a wiser choice.

One bitterly cold snowy night that winter, the neighborhood was awakened by frantic shouts of "Fire! Fire!" Etta aroused her sleepy husband, and both of them rushed to the nearest window to see the frightening sight.

"O Dan, it's the brush factory!" Flames leaped high into the black night sky, making weird shadows on the white snow.

Dan was close to tears. "My tools—all my tools. And my job, Etta—there goes my job. Now how can we make out?"

Sitting slumped on the edge of the bed, Dan was a picture of total discouragement. For days that discouragement hung on. Yet out of the ashes of the old brush shop came a new idea. Why not have a brush shop of their own? A great idea, but it was an uphill project, too. Dan located a good place for the shop, but it would mean moving their home. The house at the new location was in terrible shape, but it wasn't completely hopeless. They decided to paper the bedroom. At least one room would be clean and fresh.

Etta was delighted when she got home with her frugal purchase.

"Look, Dan!" she bragged. "The cheapest—and the prettiest, too." Proudly she displayed her choice of wallpaper.

"Squirrels, huh? And acorns among the oak leaves. What's that saying, 'Tall oaks from little acorns grow'? Well, at least it's masculine. All I need now is a rifle, and we can have squirrel potpie for dinner anytime you say the word."

"Now, Dan, don't make fun." Etta started to get ready for the painful process. "I'll paste, and you hang," she suggested.

Dan laughed. "You hang? What a way to talk to an ever-loving husband! Etta, did you ever hang wallpaper?"

"No, but I've seen it done." By this time both of them were laughing like two children. Cutting, measuring, pasting, folding, and holding. No doubt the hardest part would be the holding. Brush in hand, Dan perched himself on the top of the ladder.

"Now the fun begins," he observed. "To get this strip started straight I'll fasten it across the top first—like so. Then unfolding ve-e-ry gently, I'll free the bottom, like so. Now, my girl, will you take the brush and stroke it smoothly down to the baseboard? Wait, wait, Etta. We have a wrinkle here. Now let me loosen it a little. Oh, no!"

The whole strip pulled loose, and the top part collapsed into a tent over Dan's head. But he was undaunted.

"Now wait, dear. This is the way I used to do it. You grasp the top edge firmly. Good! Now take it up a few steps on the ladder. Fine." Dan slipped quickly out from under the paper and like a good sport climbed the ladder to start over.

"A little paste, dear. No, just hand me the paste brush." Finally the strip was stuck to the top of the wall again. Dan loosed the fold and let it fall to the baseboard.

"So far, so good." Handing the brush to Etta, he instructed, "Now, brush down the center first, and then work toward the outer——"

"O Dan! Look what I did!" The corner of the brush had punched an ugly hole in the sticky paper.

"Loosen it quick. Let it hang free."

"Honey, it's all crooked."

"Loosen it first, then brush it."

"O Dan, now see what it does!"

"I thought you knew how to hang paper."

"Well, I never actually did it before."

"You surely didn't. Now try again. Pull it loose a little, Etta. Brush it easy, dear."

Etta was annoyed. "Well, hold it straight then." This time the brush tore into the dampened paper. It was too much.

Dan said plainly, "Etta, you don't know how to paper."

In an identical tone Dan's sweet little wife answered him: "All right, do it alone then!" The door slammed as she stamped out of the room.

Minutes passed.

"Etta, Etta! Come here, dear."

The door squeaked open just a crack.

"Come on, help me, sweetheart. I'll be good." Pleading soft brown eyes looked down from the ladder. "You know I can't do it alone, and neither can you. It has to be done, so why don't we start all over with a clean strip. I'll forgive you," he finished.

"You'll forgive *me?*"

They both laughed heartily, and Etta climbed three steps on the ladder to kiss her husband. The feud was ended.

"To Be, or Not to Be"

SCHOOLTEACHER, bookkeeper, housekeeper, wife. Like the old rhyme, on it goes—seamstress, gardener, brushmaker, cook. Now that looks like quite enough accomplishments for any one woman.

But Daniel Kress's best brushmaker was being replaced, for she was adding yet another career to her long list—motherhood. To be a mother in any generation seems to be the pinnacle of a woman's career.

Parenthood is not only the soft-gowned madonna cradling a tiny bundle in the curve of her arm. It is not only a smiling father bringing huge bouquets of red roses to celebrate the exciting event. It is also that young father wondering how he will meet the bill that the doctor sends. It is his determination, regardless of the bill, to give his wife the best care in the world and to prove himself a man worthy of fatherhood.

There was a mutual feeling of awe as these two new parents gazed at the miracle of their love. They had actually been partners with God in the beautiful miracle of childbirth.

Not long after May 13, 1885, however, these rosy illusions took on the harsh glow of reality. Eva, the little one, was a colic-plagued baby. Anxious, weary days and wishful, waking nights passed too slowly. Finally the new parents, worn with worry, called a wise grandmother to the rescue.

"Why not let me take Etta and the baby home with me,

63

Dan, until we can get this child adjusted and comfortable to live with?" she suggested. Dan smiled with relief. "How can I refuse?" he said.

The house was lonely, too lonely. It was May, the beginning of the baseball season, and baseball was Dan's first love. Could any baseball lover, even a new father, allow such a chance to pass by?

Remembering his resolution to help his friends find a better way of celebrating victory after the games, and remembering that his pockets were nearly empty, Dan hurried to the nearby grocery.

What the proprietor thought when Dan bought out his whole supply of lemons and ordered more, we can only surmise. But Dan made lemonade and plenty of it, sparkling fresh and frosty cold.

The lemonade stand was a popular place, for lemonade was a good drink for children as well as adults. The afternoon's work netted him a profit of $100. Overjoyed, the new father caught the first train out of Flint, Michigan, to retrieve his small family. The empty house again echoed with the gurgles and coos of a new baby, who by now had become adjusted to life in the Kress home.

About this time Lauretta, looking through the old family Bible, noticed that Dan's father's name, Anthony Kress, was spelled with a "K." For some unknown reason, Philip, John, and Dan had been spelling their names "Cress." This puzzled Lauretta. "Why should they spell their names different from their own father?" she wondered.

Lauretta started a crusade. She began spelling her name with a "K." It was comical to see letters in the mail with the different spellings. In time, however, she won out, and Dan began to use the same spelling as his small, aggressive wife.

One evening in 1886 a special meeting was held in the First Baptist Church. The Kresses were there with little Eva. There was a divine Guest present also, for Dan's heart was influenced by the Holy Spirit. When the sermon was finished, he determined to stand to his feet and consecrate his life to his Master. Etta stood by his side with the baby sleeping in her arms. All heaven must have sung a new song that night.

As Etta and Dan walked home in the darkness, carrying their sleeping baby, Dan said thoughtfully, "I've been thinking about this pipe and the cigars I've been smoking so long, Etta. I used to think it was a manly thing, probably because so many men I knew smoked. Now, I've begun to wonder what's good about it. It smells up the house; it discolors my teeth. I kiss you and wonder how you can kiss me back. I've made up my mind to quit. Besides, I spend too much of our hard-earned cash for this silly habit. Here——" Dan reached into his pocket as they entered the house. "Take these cigars, this pipe, and the tobacco. Get them out of my sight, Etta. I'm determined to quit!"

"There's nothing I would rather do, Dan," and Etta held out both hands joyfully.

The next morning came too soon. Without his usual smoke, determined Dan kissed his wife good-bye. She smiled as he left, with a prayer on her lips as she turned to close the door.

At ten o'clock the front door's unmusical squeak announced a visitor. Surprised, Etta looked up from her work in the kitchen.

"Dan—you home?"

"Etta, where's my pipe? The cigars—where are they? I—I can't stand it any longer. I've been no good at work all morning. Please, dear. It's awful!"

"Wait a minute. Sit down, Dan. Let's talk about it."

"Etta, please. I can't take it any longer. Where did you put——"

5

Dan's wife interrupted. "But, Dan, you want to give it up——"

"Yes, dear, but I can't. That was yesterday."

"Yesterday or today—what does that matter? You know you want to win this battle, Dan. You'll only lose what you've already gained if I give them to you now. I want to help you, dear. God wants to help you. We can't give up now. Let's pray about it!"

"Pray?" Dan looked puzzled.

"Yes, sweetheart. You remember it was your mother's prayers that helped you quit drinking."

"You're right."

Lauretta looked into her husband's anxious eyes. "Where would we all be today if you hadn't stopped drinking? Now you really want to be a good Christian. We've got to go on step by step to better things, but how can we if——"

"Yes, darling. It is a filthy habit. I hate it. I don't see how you've put up with it this long."

That did it. Etta's tears overflowed. "O Dan, you'll never know how much I've prayed for you all morning! I was so happy last night to see you take your stand. We can't give up now."

"Let's pray right here."

Beside the chair they lifted their voices to God for help. This was a real struggle, a battle between good and evil. Like Jacob they pleaded for victory. "I will not let thee go, except thou bless me."

Dan arose from his knees. He took his wife in his arms. There were tears in his eyes as he spoke. "I feel so much better, darling. Where are the cigars and the pipe?"

Lauretta looked puzzled. "On our dresser," she answered.

"Go get them. I'm going to throw them into the stove."

It didn't take long for Etta to return with the items in

question. Quickly she lifted the lid of the kitchen range. In one more instant the tobacco, pipe, and cigars were part of the flames. Watching them disintegrate, Dan mused, "That's where they belonged in the first place."

The struggle was over. The victory had been won. Kissing his wife proudly, Dan walked like a new man out the front door. Turning as he crossed the lawn, he waved happily. If he could have heard her thoughts, he would have been even happier. Waving good-bye, with tears on her cheeks, she was saying to herself, "I'm so proud of you, Daniel Kress! I knew you could do it."

Bustles and Bows

BEING YOUNG in the year 1886 was a wonderfully fascinating experience. A young man on the verge of manhood grew a moustache or a beard. He wore a stiff white stand-up collar held in place by a removable button. This was duly covered with a long, wide tie. His hat was high-crowned and small-brimmed, a first cousin to the famous black derby.

Buttons and bows were high fashion for the young ladies. Large-brimmed hats were handmade. The huge draped bows, embellished with laces and ribbons, bounced along with every dainty step. Long trailing skirts swept the floors; they dusted the stairways with heavy brocaded material which trailed in pleated fullness down the back. Those were the days of the rustling silks, the tiny wasp waist, and the bustle.

Being a normal female, Lauretta Kress loved to dress up. Her fine black silk boasted many yards of cloth. It was daintily draped, pleated, and gathered. It also included a bustle.

One fine Sunday morning the Kresses were in their customary church pew. Daniel glanced proudly at his small wife, neat and trim in her new dress. She had been both the designer and the seamstress of this eye-catching creation.

But Lauretta was miserable and restless. She turned uncomfortably in her seat, first to one side and then to the other. Anxiously she looked about the church at the other women. She noticed that they too seemed restless and uncomfortable.

"These bustles may be the height of fashion, but they're also the height of misery," she decided. "Sitting through this sermon is the ultimate test of patience."

Later she told Dan, "I never heard a word that preacher said, I was so engrossed in uncomfortable clothes."

She left the service as early as she could. She hurried up the stairs at home. Pulling off the offensive dress, she threw it on the bed. Grabbing a pair of scissors, she hurriedly freed the bouncy bustle, releasing yards of flowing silk.

Holding her hard-earned material in her hand, she declared, "There's enough goods here for a whole jacket." With that she took the bustle to the stove and burned it, feeling happier than she had felt for many a day.

The Kresses had been such exceptionally good help with the projects of the Baptist Church that Dan had been asked to take the full responsibilities of the church at Davisonville, Michigan. He took no small pride in his new work as a pastor and diligently studied to show himself approved of God. Their lives had new meaning and significance now.

Lauretta had begun to study, too, for her keen, quick mind was stimulated by her new interests. Without telling Dan, she had found a new friend, who was a Bible instructor. Together they read the Gospels and studied the prophecies.

A new and startling fact became obvious to her right away. She began to understand that the seventh day of the week is the true Sabbath. It was almost frightening. Etta pondered and prayed earnestly, but she kept the light hidden in her heart.

It made her often unusually quiet. To be a minister's wife and to believe differently from his teachings was a frightening experience. A turbulent storm grew within her. How could she find peace in such a gale? What would be her anchor? The harder she rowed her own boat, the farther she seemed to get from the one she loved most. For nearly a month she had secretly kept the seventh day as the Sabbath, making feeble excuses to her husband.

That her pastor-husband was being led of God, Lauretta never questioned. To see him turn from the-man-about-town he had once been to become such a sincere Christian was proof enough of divine guidance. But for his own wife to drop his hand and start down a new path by herself—small wonder she wanted to be sure before telling Dan anything.

Dan was up early next Sunday morning to work out the last-minute details of the church program. Coming into the kitchen, he noticed Lauretta still in her everyday dress. Unconcerned, she was sitting in the rocking chair feeding the baby.

"Etta, how come you aren't ready, dear?" Dan put a warm hand on her shoulder.

"You go along, Dan. Eva must be cutting teeth. She seems a little fussy this morning. I better stay home with her."

A puzzled look crossed Dan's face, but he went on to church alone.

Sunday evening the young people of the church always had their meeting. Lauretta debated with herself. Could she disappoint her husband again? But tonight was her appointment with the Bible instructor, and she had promised to visit a sick neighbor.

"Etta, dear, are you ready?" Again the anxious look crossed Dan's face.

"Dan, I promised to call on Mrs. Allen. She isn't much better. She says she sleeps better if someone helps her walk around a bit before she goes to bed."

"Etta——" Dan's soft eyes gave his face a childish look, like a boy who was trying to keep back the tears. Taking her chin in his hand and looking straight into her eyes, he said kindly, "What's wrong, Etta? Why don't you want to go with me anymore?"

Etta could have cried. Instead she answered, "I just can't tonight, dear."

The pastor of the Baptist church was not happy with her answer, and he turned quietly away.

Hearing the door close and Dan's footsteps down the porch steps, Etta quickly dressed the baby and hurried to the Bible instructor's home for her lesson. Then as soon as she could get away, she ran to the home of her neighbor, Mrs. Allen. As she helped the old lady walk around, she kept glancing anxiously at the clock. Cutting her visit as short as she could, she ran the small distance home. Arriving just in time, she snuggled her baby into bed and was sitting in the family rocking chair casually reading the church paper when Dan walked in the front door.

"Oh, hello. You're home, Etta?" The pastor seemed surprised.

"Yes, Dan."

"Where have you been?" Dan's look was just a little suspicious.

"I told you I was going to Mrs. Allen's. I walked her around, and we visited. I just now got home and put Eva to bed."

"Then why do I have a feeling of distrust? You seem to be a different person lately, Etta. I feel as if you're not being honest with me."

"I'm sorry, Dan." Etta kissed her husband. Then turning quickly to hide the unexpected tears, she hurried to Eva's room to re-cover the baby, who was already snuggled nicely in her blankets.

But the problem did not disappear. After they had gone to bed, Dan still couldn't get it off his mind. In the darkness he opened his heart to the one he loved the most.

"Lauretta, I'm so concerned about—you and me. It's

miserable to distrust the one you love most in the world. Tell me, dear, is there something I should know?"

Etta hesitated. "Yes, Dan—but I can't tell you."

"Why?"

"Because you would be angry with me."

"Tell me, Lauretta, please." Dan sat up in bed. "I can't go on like this. I've been miserable. I promise to try to understand."

Lauretta could have cried. It would be simpler if he *were* angry. Instead she would have to hurt this man who had been so wonderful to her. It would be easy to cry, but that was not the way Lauretta did things. She was not ashamed of her Lord, or of her certainty that the Sabbath was on a different day than she had thought. She must be firm in her belief. It was not a matter for tears.

Taking a deep breath, she began: "Well, Dan, you remember the day I burned my bustle? That was the same day that I met the Bible instructor, Miss Ferry. You were trying to be a good Bible student, and I wanted to keep up with you. So I agreed to take studies from her. We have studied the Gospels and the prophecies. It's been wonderful, and I've learned that the Sabbath was never changed to Sunday. I've been trying to keep it as Christ kept it—that's all."

"That's all?" Dan sat up in bed. "That's all"—he repeated it as if to make himself believe it. He jumped to his feet. "Etta, how could you? Do you realize what you're saying? How can a minister have a wife who can't even keep the same day he keeps? Is that why you've been staying at home? Etta, how can it ever work—this way? How could you, Etta?"

Dan walked into the living room. Etta could hear him pacing back and forth. Slipping to her knees beside her bed, she poured out her plea for help.

It was very late when Dan came back to bed. His wife was

still wide awake, and her pillow was soaked with silent tears. Neither of them slept much that night.

Why did life have to be so complex, Etta wondered as she gazed into the empty darkness. Why should she have to discourage this man she was so proud of? The answer seemed as remote as eternity. The seventh-day Sabbath was right, of that Etta was sure. To back away from such an important truth was not like this personable little Christian. All through the night her untamed thoughts raced at top speed like wild horses in the forest.

Near daylight a startling thought occurred to her. What if Dan should get discouraged and go back to his old life? She shuddered in the darkness. If Dan should leave her—but, no, he would never do that. Not now. What would happen to her, and to Eva, and to the new baby already on its way? There was only one conclusion. God's hand was holding the lever of circumstances. To trust in Him was the only alternative.

Breakfast was a silent meal. No good-byes were said as Dan left. In silence Etta did the dishes. In silence she made the beds and took care of her baby. The songs that usually brightened each room were gone.

As she was peeling the potatoes for dinner, the fog suddenly lifted. It was only a little thought which peeked into her heart. "Pleasant words are as an honeycomb, sweet to the soul, and health to the bones." Proverbs 16:24. Why not cheer up and show this wonderful husband that her way of life really brought happiness?

"Husband's Favorite" could be the only title for this dinner. Quickly Etta lighted the oven. She would show Dan her love had not changed. As she was slipping an apple pie into the oven, she heard footsteps on the porch.

Slowly Dan walked into the kitchen. He looked tired and anxious.

"Etta, I'd like to talk to you." Dan waited for her to look up from the gravy she was stirring.

"Yes, Dan?" She smiled.

"I've been over to Pastor Temple's house. I told him about our situation." Dan sighed reluctantly. "He feels that you have been entangled, and if you'll go over to his place, he'll try to help you. Will you go?"

Etta didn't hesitate. "Of course—if you'll look after Eva and keep an eye on the dinner. I have your favorite, dear, and it's all in the oven."

Cleaning her hands and removing her apron, she added, "I want to do what's right, Dan; and if I'm wrong, I want to know it, too."

Dan seemed relieved. He even smiled a little.

"Change your dress, and go over. I'll stay with the baby," he said.

Mrs. Kress was received into the Temple home very graciously. The pastor began by explaining that Daniel had told him of their troubles and that he thought they could be easily untangled.

"What was responsible for your change of ideas, Mrs. Kress?" he asked.

Seeing the pastor's Bible handy on the stand, she said, "If I may use your Bible here, I think I can show you." Quickly she turned to the now-familiar texts. He found nothing to offset them. Finally, he reached in his drawer for a sermon he had once given and read it to her.

Listening closely, Lauretta said when he was through, "There wasn't one text from the Bible to support your belief. I'm more convinced than ever that there is only custom and tradition for our beliefs in keeping Sunday as God's holy day. If it isn't Scriptural, then how can you and I stand before God as our Judge, taking only the ideas of men and substituting them for His holy commands?" The pastor had no answer for her.

With her arms full of books the pastor had given her, Etta returned home. After a good meal, while the baby slept, Dan and his wife opened the books to study. Together they searched, finding only the weakest reasons for Sunday observance.

Eventually Dan went into his study alone. Etta didn't disturb him. She finished the dishes and then became absorbed in one of the pastor's books. Hearing the door open, she looked up to see Daniel standing near her chair.

"Well, have you come to any conclusions?" Her voice was tender.

"A few." He pulled up a rocker and sat down. "I'm still not convinced that you are right. I plan to keep an open mind. But in the meantime, I'm still the pastor of the First Baptist Church. There is only one way I can see to go on." Dan sighed as he slowly changed his position. "It may be a hard agreement. You can keep your Sabbaths here at home. I won't interfere if you will agree not to mention the word *Sabbath* to me. You are not to go to their meetings or have them come here. You are not to read their literature or have it in our house. I'll be happy to have you go to church with me any time, but you must not teach a class. Now if you can agree to those terms——"

Suddenly all his courage vanished, and a flood of love washed over him. All the pent-up emotions were rolled into one huge wave that engulfed them both. Dan took his wife gently into his arms.

"Etta—Etta, dear." His eyes were prisms of tears. "This has been the longest day of my life. I hope we never see another like it. What else can we do? It's the only way I can see that it will ever work out."

Lauretta's head rested on Dan's shoulder. His strong hands

caressed her hair, her cheek. It was too much. Etta wept like a child, cuddling in her husband's arms. Finally she was able to answer him. "Dan, I hope you don't think I'm being obstinate. I don't mean to be. I haven't found any Biblical reason for keeping Sunday holy. I want to be true to my God and my Creator. I love you, Dan; you know it. Nothing can ever change that, no matter what happens to us. I'll agree to your proposition. I can keep my Sabbaths here at home. Let's seal it with a kiss."

Weeks later, shortly after breakfast one Sabbath morning, Daniel came smiling into the room. He carried his best Sunday suit over his arm.

"You wouldn't mind sewing on a button for an old married man, would you, dear? It's right in the front, where it shows the most. Here's the button."

"Oh, I'm sorry, Dan. I'll be happy to fix it after the Sabbath —when the sun goes—I'll have it ready for you by tomorrow." She laughed at her own awkwardness, and leaned over quickly to kiss this lovable husband of hers.

When he had gone, she laid his coat on the bed, fastening the button with a safety pin. Kneeling there by the bed, she pleaded again to God that this fine man might see the Sabbath as she saw it, and that they might worship Him together.

The next morning the button was sewed in place. Etta went to church with her husband and listened with pride to his fine sermon. As a teacher, she was always amazed at one thing about him: Dan seldom used notes in his talks. The cup of his mind must have been so well filled that it overflowed like a clear fountain. She knew instinctively that he had a way with words, both spoken and written. There must be some great future for him in the use of words. Folding this knowledge to her heart, she prayed harder as the days passed.

In the summer, about a year from the time Etta had sealed

her bargain with Dan, the Kresses entertained a Baptist evangelist in their home. His name was Elmer Harris. This tall, pleasant man was a keen Bible student, who would eventually supply the answer to her prayers.

Because the day was sultry and hot, the two men decided to study together in the church. Coming into the small sanctuary, Pastor Harris observed the words written on a large plaque on the wall behind the pulpit. Looking up, he read aloud, " 'Remember the Sabbath Day to keep it holy.' " Walking down the aisle behind Daniel, he said, "You know, Pastor, that reminds me——"

"Yes?"

"I made a promise to one of my converts in northern Michigan. The young man was perplexed about which day is the right Sabbath—Saturday or Sunday. He wanted a Bible answer. I haven't studied into it very much, but I promised I would help him. Now, I should look it up and send him a reply." Turning to Dan, he asked, "Will you study into the question with me?"

Somewhat surprised, Dan replied, "I think I've settled that question for good. I'd rather leave it alone."

Pastor Harris chuckled. "But how would that help me? Now wouldn't you consent to help a fellow in need? Come on, Dan. This should be an interesting study. Share your findings with me."

Reluctantly Pastor Kress agreed.

When Wednesday evening came, a surprise was in store for Etta. Mr. Harris had gone up to his room early. Picking up her sewing, Lauretta began the embroidery on the tiny garments in her lap.

"Two months to go," she remarked, smiling.

"That looks very pretty, little Mother," Dan said affectionately as he stood over her chair, watching her dainty stitches.

"Thank you, Dan. I'm glad I can sew. I guess every girl feels that she is still making doll clothes when she sews for her babies. Really, this is half the fun of being a mother."

"Etta, you were never more beautiful."

"Well, thank you, kind sir. I'll remember that all my life! I love you, Daniel Kress."

Dan yawned a little. "I think I'll get to bed early, dear. Oh, by the way—don't plan on Harris and me for dinner tomorrow. We'll be at the church all day."

"For the day?" Etta could not believe her ears.

"We've decided to fast." Dan leaned down and kissed his wife. "And, remember us in your prayers, sweetheart. Good night."

Daniel was gone from the room before Etta realized what he had said. Why? Why? Etta sat up straight in her chair. "That's the first time Dan has asked me to pray for him in a whole year." Was the fog lifting? Was the sun beginning to shine through? Dare she even hope?

If she had been a church mouse, she might have had the answer; but being instead a dutiful wife, she closed the day with the same anxious prayer and laid aside her sewing. She was soon dreaming peacefully beside her sleeping husband.

Thursday evening was the prayer meeting, and of course Etta went. It was an excellent meeting. The next morning was Friday, and there was plenty to do. Dan and Pastor Harris picked a generous pailful of berries for the little cook, and after the morning meal Mr. Harris walked into the library. He picked out a book entitled *The Great Controversy Between Christ and Satan*. It was a book Lauretta's mother had given her. She had read it half through when Dan, after scanning it, forbade her to read any more of it. There was the bookmark still between the pages where she had stopped reading.

Lauretta heard Pastor Harris say, "Dan, this is the book we

need, *The Great Controversy Between Christ and Satan.* This is an exposition on Matthew 24. Suppose we just sit down here and read this."

Etta's two ears were strained to hear the answer. She did not quite catch her husband's reply, but someone was reading aloud the rest of that morning.

Busy with the Friday cleaning and the food preparation, Etta hardly noticed what was happening. She was completely absorbed in cookie making when she looked up to see Dan and Pastor Harris watching her intently.

"Etta, we think you ought to know——"

She turned quickly.

"We've been studying the Sabbath question all week."

"Really? O Dan!"

"I—I guess your prayers have been answered. We're ready to keep the Sabbath with you tonight at sunset."

"Dan! Do you really mean it?" Cookie cutter in one hand, the other smeared with flour, Lauretta circled her arms around her husband's neck. With unashamed tears she said, "I've been happy many times in my life, but not this happy, Dan!"

When Dan could speak, he said, "You have Pastor Harris to thank for this, Etta. He started it all."

"August 27, 1887, will be a date to remember, Lauretta," Pastor Harris said, beaming from ear to ear. "That makes three happy people, doesn't it? No, four," he corrected himself. "I nearly forgot my young man who asked me to write to him, but I'm sure now I'll know what to tell him."

God "Has a Thousand Ways"

$\mathcal{P}$EN IN HAND, Daniel Kress considered carefully the words he would write. He was composing his official resignation to the board of the First Baptist Church in Davisonville, Michigan. He wrote:

"August 30, 1887

"I, Daniel H. Kress, the present pastor of the First Baptist Church in Davisonville, Michigan, submit my resignation to the Board of Trustees. Because I have found and do believe that the Biblical Sabbath is the seventh day of the week, and find no Biblical reason for a change to Sunday, the first day of the week, I feel it is necessary to relinquish my post of duty as your pastor.

"Sincerely your brother,
"Pastor Daniel H. Kress"

Dan's farewell sermon spread the news like fire before a stiff breeze. Some friends in the church suggested the Kresses finish out their term and simply avoid the controversial subjects. But that was not Daniel's idea of fairness or sincerity.

After the Board of Trustees met, they informed the Kresses that because the annual term agreements had not been filled, the board felt no obligation to pay for the services already given.

After reading the notice, Dan and Etta were left a little breathless. The pay had never been regular, and their funds were very limited.

6   81

"But, Dan, how can we manage?" Etta was perplexed.

It was already August, and the new baby was due in October. It seemed the whole Red Sea had suddenly rolled in on top of them.

"We must trust, darling. God never forsakes His own. We're doing what's right. Of course Satan will make it hard for us. But God is leading, and I feel that something new and wonderful is about to happen for us. God has a thousand ways, a thousand ways.

"We have enough money to go to your folks. The furniture will have to wait. I want you and Eva to go by train right away, sweetheart."

"But, Dan, what about you?"

"It's only twenty-two miles to Flint, Etta. I'm still a good walker, and the exercise may do some good." He laughed good-naturedly.

"By the way, dear, you can take those leftover brushes with you. They should sell well in Flint. That'll tide us over until we can get started at something else. Now, I'll do the packing, and you can do all the heavy watching. You must be careful— doctor's orders, Mrs. Kress!"

"Very well, Doctor; suppose I pay for that prescription right now." Leaning forward, Etta planted a kiss where kisses belong.

Two days later Lauretta and the baby were boarding the train with their baggage. Daniel, his pockets stuffed with sandwiches and apples, took his Bible in his hand and struck out on the road leading to Flint.

"They are never alone that are accompanied with noble thoughts," the proverb says. Besides noble thoughts, faith and courage walked along the road to Flint with Daniel. A weight was suddenly lifted from his heart. He walked free and happy on his long journey into a future unknown and untried. Like

Abraham, Dan asked only that God would continue to lead as He so plainly had been leading. When Dan got tired, he would look for a cool shade tree by the roadside, where he could rest and read his Bible.

The little family was welcomed with open arms into the Eby home, and they were given two rooms to call their own. The first few meals they ate with the Ebys, but that couldn't go on. The Kresses' cupboard was very nearly bare. One morning Etta fixed some cornmeal porridge for breakfast, but that was all there was to fix. In the afternoon she and little Eva found some wild berries that would do for supper. It was a long, worrisome day, but at five o'clock God stepped into the picture. A gentleman drove his team and wagon into the Ebys' driveway. Lauretta's mother greeted the man, who was a friend of the Kresses from the Davisonville area.

"Well, Brother Jones, aren't you lost?" Lauretta asked, wondering what would bring this man so many miles to see them. "This is my mother, Mrs. Eby, Mr. Jones. That was a long trip to make just to visit us. I feel honored."

"I was plowing this morning, and everything went wrong," Mr. Jones said as he took a seat in the rocker by the window. He put his cap on his knee as he went on: "So I left the plow right where it was, unhitched the team, and said to my wife, 'Martha, I don't feel right about the way our church has treated the Kresses.' Just because you had not fulfilled your yearly contract is no reason not to pay you for what you have already done. Why, I'm a farmer, and if I hire a man for half a day, I pay him for half a day. So I said to Martha, 'Fix up some things, and I'll take them over'; so here I am. Now may I bring them in for you?"

Lauretta's eyes filled with tears. Taking his big hand in hers, she said gratefully, "You'll never know how much this means to Dan and me. We were short on funds, as you can well imagine. We're so grateful. Thank you with all our hearts. We were wondering how the Lord would work it out, and He used you and your wife. God bless you both."

"Well, we never had much money either," Mr. Jones chuckled, "but such as we have, we can share." He brought into the room a bushel of potatoes, two quarts of pickles, a bushel of apples, a bag of flour, five dozen eggs, five pounds of butter, and two loaves of freshly baked bread, brown and crusty. Lauretta felt like Mary, the mother of Jesus, as the Wise Men brought the gifts which were later used to sustain them in the land of Egypt.

The little family held a praise service that night before the delicious meal was eaten. Two hungry adults and one little girl knew the loving care of God for His children, for they had felt the warmth of His hand as they walked on in faith to obey Him. Dan and Etta were together at last, in all the ways of their lives. Together they walked with God, who would lead them in paths they could scarcely imagine.

One day about a month later, Etta was looking over the winter clothing for the family when she discovered a need. Dan's overcoat looked shabby. Winter comes early to Michigan, so Etta decided to do the only thing she knew which would help the situation. Turning the coat inside out, she found that the inside looked colorful and neat. Why not rip the seams and turn it completely?

It was a huge task. Being a good seamstress was a paying profession; but as the job neared completion, the seamstress encountered a few unexpected complications.

"Mother," she called from the top of the stairs, "come here, will you? I was wondering why I didn't feel quite up to par today. Now I know."

Mrs. Eby asked knowingly, "The baby?"

Lauretta nodded. "Before Dan's overcoat is done, too. Here

comes another pain! Mother, we better get things ready. You'll find everything in the closet there on the first shelf." Etta stopped long enough to hug her mother affectionately. "What would the world do without good mothers?" she added.

Having a baby in those days meant a home delivery, with a faithful mother or a kind neighbor to help. Few expectant mothers went to the hospitals, mostly because there were very few hospitals.

Time seemed like eternity. Elastic moments were stretched to the breaking point. No one but a mother can know the heights of joy or the depths of fear in this cavern of pain where there is no turning back.

The helpless moments usually dreaded by a father were spared to Daniel Kress this time, for when he arrived home from a short trip to Flint, the new baby, Ora, was safely tucked in the circle of her mother's arm. And Lauretta, tired but happy, looked up from her bed to welcome the surprised father.

Dan, wide-eyed with the wonder of it all, was amazed by two miracles: one, the new baby; the other, the new winter coat. Who could blame him for remarking tenderly to his small mate, "Etta, how do I deserve such a wonderful wife?"

Opening Doors

OPENING DOORS—the rough-hewn doors of pioneer cabins, the well-painted doors of mansions in the city, the heavy utilitarian doors of factories, hospitals, schools, and businesses of every kind. There were plain doors and artistic doors, doors of new churches and new colleges. All of these could be unlatched by the finger of ambition.

Just before the turn of the century as the nation was completing its expansion westward, there was great optimism and hope. The country was again united following the Civil War and its aftermath. The promise of better days ahead stirred men and women to new activities of all kinds, and the atmosphere itself seemed charged with challenge. Success was possible for anyone who was willing to try for it.

"If you can make a better mousetrap, make it!" seemed to be the slogan of the hour. Another motto, "Go west, young man, go west," had been amplified to say, "Go south, go east —just go, go, go—and do something constructive when you get there."

Into this age came Lauretta and Daniel Kress. Hand in hand they faced the future. Like many others, they stood at a door that opened abruptly before them.

"Etta, Etta dear, where are you?" Dan called from the front porch of their home.

"Dan, are you home already?"

"Yes, dear! I told you I felt something good was about to happen. Look! It's happened!"

Dan reached into his pocket and pulled out a handful of paper money, stiff and crackly. "Fifty dollars!" he announced with a chuckle. "Our good friend Mark insisted I take it as a loan. He knew I wanted to go to Battle Creek for that special course. Imagine—me a college student!"

"Mr. Collegiate!" Etta congratulated Dan with a warm kiss. "How nice of Mark! It's exactly what you need to help with your ministerial work. O Dan, isn't God good to us?"

"Indeed He is. But, Etta, I hate to leave you and the children, even for a few weeks."

"You're not to worry, Pastor Kress. I'm still handy with my needle, and we'll make out fine. Your job is to walk into this open door that God has provided. When I think of how God has led you and me to where we are today, I can't ever do enough for Him in return."

"You're right, dear, of course. Help me pack my suitcase, will you?"

In July of the same year another door opened almost majestically. This was more of a portal than a door, for it had the dignity of a church.

Dan had returned from his ministerial retreat at Battle Creek. Life again moved along at an even, peaceful pace for a while. But it was soon camp meeting time in Michigan.

"This time I insist." It was Dan's voice. "You're going to your first Seventh-day Adventist camp meeting, Etta. I had my turn, you know; now it's yours. I can stay here with the children. Besides, you need a rest." Dan didn't often put his foot down; but when he did, it usually stayed down. Etta went off to camp meeting.

One day soon after the session began, Etta had a spine-tingling surprise. As she was walking to her tent after a meeting, a pleasant-faced gentleman spoke to her: "O Mrs. Kress, there you are! Someone told me you were on the grounds, and I've been looking for you. I have some money I have owed your husband for a long time. He did a good job for me, and I never have paid him for it. Here you are."

The man reached into his pocket and, producing his wallet, counted out the money into her hand. "That's twenty, thirty, forty, and fifty. The name is Judson—Will Judson. Do tell your husband hello for me." And he shook her hand eagerly.

"Thanks—thank you so very much!" A little dazed, like a child getting off a merry-go-round, Etta stood stiff and motionless with the loose bills in her hand.

When the man was out of sight, Etta thought, "Now here's fifty dollars, just what I need to pay off Mark for his loan to Dan."

The little dreader of debts immediately found her friend and paid him in full. Happily clinging to her receipt, Etta walked past the conference office on her way back to her tent.

Suddenly she noticed one of the pastors motioning to her from the window. She hurried inside.

"Come in, Mrs. Kress." The inviting voice was full of cheer. "I have something here for your husband. Would you take it to him? You're now the wife of a licensed Seventh-day Adventist minister. Here's the document, all signed and sealed. May God richly bless you both." The man smiled as he handed the large envelope to Etta.

His words rang like a sweet-toned carillon all through the rest of that wonderful camp meeting. They were still echoing like church bells when Etta returned home to her pastor-husband.

At last the Kress family was settled. Dan's work as a pastor was satisfying and remunerative. The salary was sure and regular. They carefully budgeted their $7.50-a-week allotment.

With the added wealth of a home garden, they managed well. What more could a young couple want, they wondered. Then it happened!

Without a flourish another door opened. Lauretta was taking a cooking class taught by Mrs. E. E. Kellogg. She had enjoyed every minute of it. On the last day Dan had come to get his cook and take her home. The good-byes were said, and Dan's hand was already on the doorknob as they were leaving.

But another hand was on the same knob! It was the hand of Dr. J. H. Kellogg.

"Well, well, how do you do? Now this would be——" The little doctor was speaking, shaking first Dan's hand, then Etta's.

Mrs. Kellogg spoke: "Doctor, this is Mrs. Kress, my student, and her husband Pastor Kress. This is Dr. J. H. Kellogg."

Dr. John Harvey Kellogg was called the czar of the Battle Creek Sanitarium. It was an awesome experience for the Kresses to meet this head surgeon. Etta did not miss a single feature of this famous man, from his limited height to his bald head that glowed in the sunlight as he invited them to be seated. Leaning eagerly over his desk, he smiled in his warm, quick way. His neat moustache drew their eyes to his meticulously well-trimmed goatee, which seemed to make his round face come to a decided point. But his personality was his crowning feature.

"I hear you have been an exceptional student, Mrs. Kress."

"Really?"

"Yes, ma'am; and we're looking for exceptional students. In fact," he continued, "we will settle for just plain students. We need doctors desperately!"

"Doctors?" Lauretta's voice betrayed her surprise.

"Yes, I mean it. You would make a fine obstetrician, and, Pastor, your ministerial training and experience could link right into the medical work. That's the way the Master did it!

A perfect combination. Perfect!" There was that smile again, drawing like a magnet. When the first words had penetrated, the doctor continued, "Now, what do you think about it—both of you?"

Lauretta looked at Dan and smiled weakly.

"It—it's a little frightening," Dan managed. "We—we have just this summer gotten ourselves settled."

"Settled?" The doctor took the word out of Daniel's mouth. "That's not a good word, Pastor. Youth is always ready to make a change, especially in our work. The work must go forward—forward." He leaned forward as he spoke, more earnest than before. "Think of all the good a pair of doctors could do! We have a fine sanitarium here, yes—but this is only the beginning. We need such hospitals all over the world." His short arms outstretched to encompass the whole earth. "All these institutions will need fine young doctors—to teach, to lecture, to supervise, to practice. We need nurses. Who will train them? Come now—let me sign you both up for the fall session!"

Dr. Kellogg opened a drawer. He produced a pad of paper. Dipping the pen in the ink, he held it out to Dan. "We're starting our first class in September. The first year will be right here on our campus and the last three years at Ann Arbor, Michigan. Last year the medical course was a three-year training, but this year the four-year plan begins. It's going up, folks! You better join now," he urged.

"We want God to lead," Dan said. "We have a family, you know. Two children make a difference."

"Two children are a great asset. You're a rich man. We can work that out all right." The doctor waited anxiously for their reaction.

Dan's eyes sought his wife's response. Then he said, "Etta would make a fine doctor, and I wouldn't object for myself, if the Lord is leading us into this work. I'd be willing except for one thing."

"What's that?" The doctor's eyes were sharp.

"That's the two hundred dollars I still owe!"

"Two hundred?" The doctor stood up behind the desk.

"I owe it to the conference for the ministerial course I've just finished," Dan explained.

In his own nervous, quick way the doctor said, "And that's all that stands between you folks and school?"

Etta looked a bit puzzled. "We shun debts like a plague," she explained. "Doctor, I don't see how we could add another debt to the one we already owe."

Dr. Kellogg acted like a man with a fish on his line. He sat down. He pressed a buzzer. Almost instantly a callboy stood at attention. When the doctor finished writing a short note, he put it in the boy's hand. "Take this to the manager's office, and hurry back with the answer. Thanks, Jim."

After the door closed, the doctor paced the floor. He had ideas, definite ideas. This one possessed him completely. "I can see an army of youth. Those are Mrs. White's own words," he declared. "An army of youth marching into our schools as students, then marching out as workers—trained workers, efficient and dedicated."

The doctor stopped in front of Daniel as he spoke: "You young people will step into the most important work. You'll be the pioneers—in this country, in every country. The world is the field." The old clock on the wall ticked loudly. It seemed to repeat, "The field, the field, the field." Then the doctor went on. "Church schools, academies, colleges, seminaries—who knows? Maybe a university! See what I mean? Time is wasting." Again the clock reiterated, "Wasting, wasting, wasting."

The doctor was urgent. "We want a large class this year so that we'll have a good beginning. The first year will be here—or did I tell you that? The subjects will be anatomy, bacteriology, hygiene, and Bible. The university will give us full credit. You have heard of the good Dr. Mayo? Will Mayo graduated from Ann Arbor in 1883. This is the day of opportunity—open doors." Again that clock repeated, "Open doors, open doors, open doors!"

The door swung open suddenly, like a cue in a play. Jim, the callboy, handed Dr. Kellogg a note. Scanning its contents, the doctor's face brightened like that of a small boy. "Good! Good! Thank you, Jim. That will be all. Now, Daniel and Lauretta Kress, this note informs me that I may pay off your indebtedness to the conference of two hundred dollars. Here is the check." With a happy flourish, the doctor handed the pen, freshly dipped in ink, to Daniel.

"But—Doctor," Dan stammered, "how can you do that?"

"I'm happy to do it! We need you two fine young people, and God needs you."

"Thank you, Doctor. We do understand." It was Etta, reaching her hand for the pen. Dr. Kellogg had worked hard for that signature and the one that followed. The thanks were said again, and the good-byes. The names were transferred to the student roster for the fall term. With a feeling of strange exhilaration the Kresses found themselves in the hall.

"Well—Dr. Daniel Kress," Etta said, and laughed.

"Well—Dr. Lauretta!" Dan laughed as he kissed his happy wife. "I never thought when we came in that door that we would come out as prospective college students. One never knows what's behind a closed door."

The Bridge to Tomorrow

*W*E BID thee farewell!" Lauretta Kress laughed as she reached out to pat the door casing affectionately.

"Come on, Etta; let's go." Daniel looked tired.

"Now, don't 'come on, Etta' me, Daniel. I want to tell this room good-bye properly before we leave," she insisted.

"We've lived a whole year here in Battle Creek," she went on. "We've studied and slept and eaten our fill"—at that thought she laughed, remembering—"with two of us sitting on the side of the bed and the other two on the only two chairs we had! We've even lived on our budget—two and a half cents a meal. Of course that meant granose biscuit, day-old bread, apples at fifteen cents a bushel, potatoes at twenty—but you know, Dan, we haven't been sick a day, not a one of us!

"I congratulate you, Daniel Kress, for your patience with me, in this one room. And you, Eva and Ora, you've both been good girls. May God bless the next tenants. I hope they'll be as happy as we have been."

Then Etta stooped to take little Ora in her arms and pick up the baggage that was hers to carry.

"To Ann Arbor, girls! Now we're real university students. What do you think of that?"

"Me, too, Mamma?"

"Why, of course, you too!" Dan agreed as he shepherded his little flock to the livery that waited outside.

Their destination was 21 East Jefferson Street, Ann Arbor, Michigan. This residence home had been especially purchased by the Battle Creek Sanitarium as a dormitory for their medical students. Lauretta was assigned to be the matron, and Dan would act as dean of men and residence chaplain.

Twenty students signed the collegiate roster that first year. New Zealand, Ontario, Australia, Arkansas, New York, Maine, New Brunswick, Michigan, Kansas, and Minnesota were represented. What a melting pot!

Into this caldron were poured the varied human emotions of many lands. There were unusual customs, ways of life, homesicknesses, heartaches, and ambitions.

The long table in the dining room could tell many tales of fun and frolic, tears and troubles, yet it kept its secrets. A small charge of $2.50 a week for each student was made for room and board. Each student was required to work at least one hour a day. One young man, for instance, pushed a wheelbarrow one and a half miles every day to bring a large can of milk to the kitchen. Two hot meals a day were served; and fruit, milk, and crackers were available if anyone desired supper.

But one day things began to happen. The caldron of circumstances boiled over! The heavy lid, steadily pressured by human emotions, suddenly lifted and crashed to the floor right at Etta's feet. The cook had left!

Like a ship in full sail, Etta entered the kitchen and rang the bell to call the crew together.

"Come on, girls; let's get this kitchen organized. This challenge should be stimulating. You know, when I was first married, I had never cooked a meal in my life. What a struggle we had!" She shook her head.

"Now, I've listed the menu on the blackboard. You can work in teams, and we'll rotate. The men will have to take their turns, too." The group listened doubtfully.

"But we have a problem," Etta went on. "Evening is our only study period; so we'll have Mary read our assignments aloud, since she is a good reader. This will mean working quietly with as few interruptions as possible. For you professional potato peelers we have a real treat tonight—baked potatoes tomorrow."

"Oh, good! We'll be done in no time."

Lauretta smiled. "Here are the scrub brushes. I can't stand gritty potatoes, and"—she slid a huge pan of carrots in their direction—"when you've finished the potatoes, work on these." Amid sighs of disappointment Mary began reading.

"Our first assignment concerns the emblem used by the medical world, the caduceus. It has an interesting meaning. 'It comes from a Greek word which means a staff of an ancient herald. The two wings signify speed. The serpents coiled around the staff are also meaningful. They point to the time of Moses. When the children of Israel were not grateful for God's protection, He allowed venomous serpents to overrun the camp. Many people were bitten and died painful deaths. Then God commanded Moses to make a brass serpent and raise it up on a pole. All who came and looked upon it were healed.

" 'So what does the caduceus symbolize? The doctor is a staff, to guide, to lean upon, and to lift up Christ in His work. Only God could heal the serpent's bite, and only He can heal today. When we as doctors fail to lift Him up and take the glory of a patient's healing for ourselves, we are no longer worthy to wear the caduceus, for it will have lost its meaning.'

"The next part of our lesson is as important to a doctor as the Florence Nightingale pledge is to a nurse. This is the Hippocratic oath. We are to memorize this, so I have copied one for each of us to take along. Follow along with me as I read it, and find in each part an ideal that you want for yourself as a doctor of today.

7

The Oath of Hippocrates

" 'I do solemnly swear, by whatever I hold most sacred:

" 'That I will be loyal to the profession of medicine and just and generous to its members;

" 'That I will lead my life and practice my profession in uprightness and honor;

" 'That into whatsoever house I shall enter, it shall be for the good of the sick to the utmost of my power, holding myself far aloof from wrong, from corruption, from the tempting of others to vice;

" 'That I will exercise my profession solely for the cure of my patients, and will give no drug, perform no operation, for a criminal purpose, even if solicited; far less suggest it;

" 'That whatsoever I shall see or hear of the lives of men which is not fitting to be spoken, I will keep inviolably secret.

" 'These things do I swear.

" 'And now, should I be true to this, my oath, may prosperity and good repute be ever mine; the opposite, should I prove myself forsworn.' "

Thus the lessons were learned. Each evening's study period was flavored with aromas of the good wholesome meals that were to be served the next day.

Examination periods were times of particular stress and consternation. Different methods of study were used.

Tonight there is a stir in the kitchen. Lauretta Kress, spoon in hand, is making an interesting announcement:

"Since tomorrow is examination day, I've asked for a little help from the men. Mr. Kress and his group of fellows will review the important highlights of medical growth from 1600 to the present. Come right in, gentlemen."

Lauretta moved back to her worktable in her usual way, but not so with the others. A feminine eyebrow lifted. A busy hand hastened to arrange a stray lock of hair or to tie a neater bow on an apron.

The men found seats in any handy place. In his slow, quiet way, Dan stood and began to speak.

"You young ladies are not to be distracted from your work, we hope, but we felt this is a small way to repay you for all the good meals you have served us. Right, fellows?"

Enthusiastic applause ensued.

Then Daniel continued: "Each of us has a part assigned to review. William, here, from Australia, will speak about a man with the same name as his and the same British accent. Whom do I mean, girls?"

"William Harvey!" came the quick response.

Shuffling a handful of papers, William slowly eased to his feet and began:

"Well, first, I have a mental picture of this man Harvey. May I share it with you? I would note first his British accent, as Mr. Kress has said, and feel right at home with him. He'd be a bit taller than I am and have snow-white hair. When he looked at me, I would see a pair of serious eyes, dark and almost piercing.

"Dr. Harvey trained at Padua University in Italy in 1600. I liked his description of the anatomical theater at the school. It was horseshoe shaped and had six tiers of seats. He says every student could see the object of study.

"Now how was he any different from the hundreds of other medics in his day? First, he was inquisitive. This led him to doubt his superiors, which was not an accepted thing to do. Galen's popular theory of the human blood circulation did not sound logical to him. He thought, 'Galen dissected only dead animals. I want to see inside a *living* body. No use; I can't even use a dead human body. But there are fish, sheep, dogs—all kinds of creatures.

" 'I wonder how much blood is in the body. Where does it go from the heart? How does it go? How much blood is pushed out in one heartbeat? If each beat ejects two fluid ounces, and there are seventy-two beats a minute——'

"So William Harvey questioned, studied, and learned. This amazing muscle, the heart, could lift every hour three times the average body weight of an adult.

"Dr. Harvey found and proved to the medical world that the blood circulates in a circle. This doctor I like," William declared. "He is real to me. I want to be his kind of doctor, dedicated to my work and to my Creator. It's a privilege to follow in his steps."

Someone said aloud, "Amen," and William took his seat.

The professional peelers took a deep breath and suddenly realized they were still holding the same carrot in their hands that they had started peeling when William began to talk. Hastily they began peeling again.

"Thank you, William. You've made Dr. Harvey a real person to us all. Now our faithful milkman, David, will tell us about the flea glasses."

Tall, lanky David Paulson unwound his long extremities and faced his captive audience.

"This story suits me fine," he began. "It's about the luckiest boy in Holland in the late 1600's. He was lucky because he had a smart father. Today we would call him an optician, but then Mr. Janssen was called a spectacle maker. One day he and his son, Zacharias, made a glass to magnify ten times. The boy was thrilled. He found a flea on his dog, speared it on a needle, and promptly showed it to his mother. 'Look in my "flea glass," Mother,' he said, holding it close.

" 'Oh, horrors, Zachy! It looks like a monster! I can see the hair on his legs!' she cried.

"Before another century Zacharias Janssen's flea glasses became a real magnifying tool. Not ten times did they magnify, but two hundred and three hundred times the size of the object.

"Then Robert Hooke of England took over. He made a very modern-looking microscope. Here was a real challenge. When a doctor asked, 'What does a blood vein look like?' the answer was clear: 'Look and see!' 'What does a drop of blood look like? a dog's kidney, a sheep's liver, an artery, a capillary?' The answer echoed like a shout against a canyon wall: 'See for yourself. Try it.'

"Seeing for himself, another physician by the name of Marcello Malpighi was to answer his hidden curiosity. He followed Harvey's circulation ideas. He found the arteries, the veins, and then came a labyrinth of capillaries. He was trapped. Where did that artery go? How did the blood get into an organ? He was too fascinated to sleep. Like a kaleidoscope it changed. Whatever would he have done without the Dutchman's flea glass? Then he saw it! The veins ran into smaller channels of blood, as fine as the hairs on his head, yet they carried blood to the end of the fingers, to the toes, to the skin, feeding and nourishing. He called them capillaries. Carefully he examined the lung, the spleen, the kidneys, the liver, and drew pictures of everything he saw.

"At the next meeting of the Royal Society he reported his findings to the medical group. 'Look,' he said to the amazed crowd; 'see this, and this, and this. The whole world must know —not only the doctors of every land, but the old folk, the young people, the children in school. Can't you see why I couldn't sleep? How must a Creator feel to have intelligent people made in His likeness so ignorant of their own bodies? Learn, learn, and never stop learning!' he admonished.

"What a foundation these men gave us to build on!" David exclaimed. "As a future physician of 1891, I stand here astonished at what we can do with the great advantages we have in our age. I dedicate myself to build a sturdy foundation for those who follow after me."

Daniel Kress's face was serious as he spoke again. "These reports are excellent, men. Now, Eric has a European background, and I thought he would like to report on smallpox and the birth of vaccination."

"Yes, sir." Eric's blond hair shone in the light that hung near the stove. "First I want to discuss the plague called smallpox. Years ago this was the great killer that stalked every country—the igloos in Alaska, the wigwams of American Indians, the bamboo huts of the Orient. No corner of the earth was free from this killer. We cannot imagine the horror of smallpox. In Europe it claimed hundreds of thousands annually. In 1796, 30,000 people died in Prussia alone. In the eighteenth century it sent at least 60,000,000 people to their graves.

"Then came the conquering hero, Edward Jenner. This 'David' had only a tiny bit of virus on the tip of his spear when he slaughtered his giant.

"Edward was cursed by some, blessed by others, yet nothing stopped him. He proved to the world he was right. He was one of the few heroes who was honored in his own lifetime. Napoleon said of him, 'We can refuse nothing to that man.'

"Edward Jenner was called 'a savior of the world.' Five nations of Indians, grateful for the freedom from smallpox, sent him a most touching tribute of gratitude. The British Parliament granted him an award of 10,000 pounds (approximately $40,300 U.S.). He was honored by the king of Spain and the emperor of France.

"The empress of Russia wrote him a letter of thanks and sent him a ring studded with diamonds. She decreed that the first child vaccinated in Russia would be named 'Vaccinoff,' and that he was to be educated with funds from the imperial treasury."

When Eric finished his account, there were tears in his eyes. "I have heard my grandparents talk of smallpox. I wish I could thank Edward Jenner, too."

"Thank you, Eric," exclaimed the lady at the stove. Lauretta Kress was taking off her apron. She turned to the group. Standing tall as her small stature would allow, she was every inch the teacher.

"I was given the next subject, because I am a mother, and perhaps as a mother I could better understand the lesson on Childbed Fever or Septicemia. It's an amazing fact that but a few years ago it was actually dangerous to become a mother. If I had been an expectant mother in 1860, or if any of you had been and had come to Dr. Ignaz Philipp Semmelweis for delivery, we would have uttered the same cry that he heard every day. 'Please, sir, assign me to the midwives' ward.'

" 'But,' he asked, knowing the answer, 'why should you want to be delivered by an ignorant midwife when you can have a medical doctor?'

"We would all answer as she did: 'Everybody knows, sir; and I don't want to die!'

" 'I don't want to die!' The words dogged his every step. Semmelweis vowed he would make motherhood safe for all mothers. He studied; he pondered; he prayed; he made records of everything. One chart read thus:

" 'A. In 6 years, Doctors' Ward, 1,989 mothers died (nearly one a day).
" 'B. In 6 years (same years), midwives, 691 mothers died.
" 'C. In Paris Dien Hospital more than half died.
" 'D. In Berlin, one out of three.
" 'E. In Keil, one out of four.
" 'F. In Jena—all died.'

"No wonder Dr. Semmelweis was in a fog. Only recently had medical men included obstetrics in their training. The midwives still proudly held a better record when it came to fatalities due to infection or puerperal fever. Most doctors simply accepted this horrible fact. 'We'll always have childbed fever,' they said, and turned away from anxiety concerning it. They didn't consider prevention possible.

"Only recently could medical men use human bodies to study. Now it was the vogue to spend part of each day in the morgue doing postmortems. Sanitary conditions were anything but good, and real cleanliness was literally nonexistent. But one day something shook the medical world. A doctor died of septicemia! He was a friend of Dr. Semmelweis's.

"Impossible! A man having the same infection as a mother! No, no! Yet here were the same symptoms, same fever, same awful agonizing death. This friend of Dr. Semmelweis's had nicked his finger as he did a postmortem. Like a knife cutting into his own heart, Semmelweis knew. He knew the same suppuration that could bring death to a mother was carried to his friend on that scalpel. The same infection could be carried on the hands of the doctor who worked in the morgue and who later examined the patient before delivery.

"He walked the floor, moaning. 'Hands, hands, hands that should bring life are bringing death to healthy mothers. O God! Could my hands, *my hands*—no, no!' Like a madman Semmelweis made his unusual announcement to his doctors. With bated breath and accusing finger he finished with these words: 'I, myself, have been the means of bringing death to a great many women, healthy women. God forgive!'

"Then came the order: 'Wash the hands. Scrub with soap!' the death rate dropped, but not enough. 'Wash with chlorine solution. Clean the fingernails, and pass for inspection.' The death rate dropped again.

"One day the students lingered over the hand washing. 'With respect, doctor, this hand scrubbing is humiliating!'

"Another added, 'Some of us are undergraduates, sir. Many are already doctors.'

" 'We're not schoolboys,' another called out.

"Another added, 'As you know, sir, the midwives line up every morning to have their nails inspected. We're not midwives! Your hypothesis is still unproved.'

"Dr. Semmelweis was silent. Then he burst forth, 'Enough! It is I who am ashamed. I have treated you as equals. Now I speak as your superior. I am responsible for every death in this ward. You will do as I say or leave. Go to Berlin, where one of three die, or to Jena, where they all die! Go where you like, but here you wash your hands!'

"Dr. Semmelweis kept his vow. Motherhood was made safe. Childbed fever disappeared from the world."

Lauretta Kress added enthusiastically, "We have come a long way since this experience. Yet today in 1891 there are still doctors who refuse to scrub their hands or boil their instruments. May God help us to vow, as Dr. Semmelweis did, to make childbirth safe for every mother. Personally I want to learn this lesson so well that no patient shall die because of my carelessness or unconcern, for it can still happen in our day. God forbid! It is up to each of us."

Etta laid aside her notebook, donned her apron, and took her place by the kitchen stove again.

In the doorway there was a stir. Three men appeared to the group. One wore a sign that read "Louis Pasteur." Another read "Dr. Robert Koch" and still another "Dr. Joseph Lister." Daniel spoke first.

"Tell me, Dr. Lister, how did you prove that microbes or germs cause infection?"

"I saw them in the microscope," replied "Lister." "I copied pictures and told everyone I could."

"You did many things. I hear one thing you did was to

wear a spotlessly clean linen apron to do surgery. But that was not accepted by all doctors. Tell us what they usually wore."

"Well, the only correct garb—to the surgeons, that is—was a frock coat. It had to be the oldest and the shabbiest in his wardrobe. It was kept in the doctors' dressing room and never cleaned or changed during twenty years of operating work. The ligatures, like a badge of knighthood, were worn in the button-hole of the frock coat—a filthy habit."

"What happened when you insisted that the ligatures and linens be clean and boiled?"

"We had to prove that boiling kills germs. Most instruments were carried in a dirty red velvet case and used just as they were. Most of the doctors didn't love me for proving these things, but some did. Here's one." "Lister" took "Dr. Koch" by the arm as he asked, "Remember the day you showed them the tubercle bacillus?"

"Yes, yes," Koch answered. "Some said, 'Lister is baloney.' They winked and mocked, but some saw and believed. Tell them about your 'donkey engine' for the operating room, Lister."

"I found that carbolic acid was a germicidal. I proved it killed germs; so we made a spray machine, and we used it. We washed everything with carbolic first, then we sprayed continuously during surgery."

"Wasn't it wet and hard to work with?" Dan asked.

"Of course, but that's better than infection."

"Mr. Pasteur, you haven't had a chance to say a word," Dan said.

"That's all right. I'm not a doctor, but a scientist. But"—"Pasteur" laughed heartily—"I was in the fight with these men, and I can tell you the air was full of controversy as well as carbolic acid. Lawson Tait was one who had determined never to open an abdomen because the results he saw were all fatal —peritonitis, then death. But he changed his mind."

"Really? Sounds like progress."

"It was. He saw their demonstration and believed. However, they weren't all like Tait. Someone started on childbed fever as usual, saying it was to be expected. I got angry, I guess, so I told them it was microbes or germs that cause infection and death, and that they were carried on the hands of doctors and nurses to the patient.

"Someone doubtingly said, 'I fear that a microbe will never be found.'

"I stepped up to the board and drew a diagram of the chainlike organisms, and I proved it with my own microscope. It was a good fight and worth all we put into it."

Dan nodded in agreement. "We will let all our future doctors here decide that for themselves. Thank you, men. You've all done a noble job tonight. Girls, please put a few extra potatoes in the soup for tomorrow. We'll all be starving hungry after those exams."

Prisoners of Promise

*W*HEN Lauretta Kress put her foot down, it usually stayed down. But one particularly bright summer morning someone else had put his foot down too, and it refused to budge.

Armed with his most winning smile, Dr. J. H. Kellogg approached the tiny office near the kitchen on the Michigan campgrounds. He observed the notice neatly posted on the door, which said "Kitchen Supervisor." He knocked gently.

Behind the small desk, planning the menus for the day, sat the dark-haired, sharp-eyed supervisor.

To her friendly "Come in," the doctor responded.

"Dr. Lauretta Kress, I believe." His warm smile sparkled as he held out his hand.

Lauretta stood up quickly as she greeted not one dignitary but two, for Elder Olsen had joined the doctor at the door. She concealed her surprise.

"How nice to see you both! Won't you be seated? I'm sorry to be so rushed here this morning, but I can spare a few minutes. This is a huge undertaking—you understand, I'm sure."

The men were seated. "Yes, yes, of course, Dr. Lauretta. But it's important that we talk to you, Doctor."

Lauretta's quick wit matched that of her visitors. Smiling, she remarked, "That's three times you have called me doctor." She seemed a little annoyed. "It's a bit premature, you know."

"Of course, I know; but it does sound good, now doesn't it?

I've been hearing things about you that I don't want to hear."

"Yes?"

"Definitely. It's true then? You have planned to discontinue your medical course, Mrs. Kress?"

"Definitely!" Lauretta borrowed the doctor's word. "All last year we had problems with the children. It isn't fair to them for me to be away so much. They really need me. I can't bear to see them running around without the proper supervision. That's just not right. As a mother I have a responsibility. With this job they can be here with me. Besides, it has been a real financial burden. This way Dan can finish easily."

"Well, now, is that the only trouble—really?" The doctor's face brightened. "There's no problem here," he stated flatly. "As for the finances, we can arrange a loan for you. If you could understand how desperately we need you young people! Mrs. Kress, you have so much potential. God needs you!

"Look ahead a few years." The doctor had a faraway gleam in his eye. "If you could see the need as I see it! We need medical personnel, teachers, pioneers in every field. We'll need a whole army of trained young people, but who will train them? We need a medical school, but where will we get the teachers? We need hospitals, in this country and in other countries. Who will take charge of them? The field is the whole world, Mrs. Kress." In his enthusiasm Dr. Kellogg had jumped to his feet.

Lauretta blushed guiltily. "You're right, Doctor; but my children—if I could get someone adequate. There's only one person I can think of that I'd have as a governess, and she's already employed at the Haskell Home."

The doctor took the hook like a hungry fish. "You mean Mattie Myers, of course. She is excellent!" Dr. Kellogg shook Lauretta's hand. "You'll hear from me tomorrow," he promised. "You see now how easily the problems work out? Elder Olsen here has been praying as we talked. He couldn't have gotten a word in edgewise anyhow," he added jubilantly. "We'll plan for you and Daniel to be on the campus this fall, Dr. Lauretta."

There was that jovial smile again and the twinkle in the eye. "I'm glad we interrupted you at your work here behind the lines. But God wants you out in front, right on the firing line. May I shake the hand of a pioneer?" Dr. Kellogg certainly had a way with words.

Elder Olsen took Lauretta's small hand in his, and looking down at the efficient little lady, he said sincerely, "It's been a pleasure to see your response. May God richly bless you for this decision."

The interview was nearly forgotten in the avalanche of work that descended upon Lauretta Kress the following day. To supervise three meals a day for this huge camp of hungry people was no small task. Little did this petite pioneer realize that even this experience would someday be a most valuable asset.

"Telegram for Mrs. Daniel Kress." Lauretta heard her name called above the bustle of noises. Wondering anxiously who of her family could be ill, she tore open the envelope. Then her eyes caught the familiar Battle Creek identification. She read, "Mattie Myers released for your help. Will leave October 2. Arrangements made for loan. Write. Dr. J. H. Kellogg."

Etta stood transfixed. Yesterday she had put her foot down. Today she was ready to walk ahead into an unknown future. Somehow the words of yesterday rang in her happy mind. A jubilant voice repeated, "May I shake the hand of a pioneer?"

* * * * *

"Spring is in the air!" Etta announced, sniffing deeply. "I feel a new awakening, as if—well——"

Dan chuckled. "As if spring is in the air!" Gathering up his textbooks, he added, "Etta, I think you ladies must have had a balmy class meeting. Tell me what you decided."

"You mean about the graduation dresses, of course. Well, you could figure it out in one guess! Everyone will wear whatever she pleases. Evelyn has vision of lavender and lace—with a train!"

Dan laughed boyishly. "A lavender train?" he asked.

"Oh, certainly. 'Women doctors should still be women,' Evelyn insists. As for me, I've decided on a new black silk with some white lace for the feminine touch. Even married ladies must be feminine, you know."

"You always look good to me. I'm glad you can sew, Etta. How would we ever have made out with two girls if you couldn't?"

The arms of a happy wife encircled her husband. "You say the nicest things, Dan."

"And why not? Every nice thing I've ever done for you has come back to me with frosting on it. How do I rate such a wife?" Dan kissed her fondly. Then he opened his textbook and lined up several pages of handwritten notes. "I'm glad school is nearly over," he said. "Tell me, Etta, how did you make out on your research of the post-Lister period?"

"I'm all finished! Let me see yours!"

"No, no, dear. I've barely started. Well, on second thought, here, look it over. I decided to make mine a sort of medical news bulletin of happenings since the Lister period began. I've been reading some on the Mayo family in Rochester, and I thought that would make a good news item too. How does it sound to you?"

"I like your news items," Etta remarked after reading what Dan had handed her, "but they make my efforts sound elementary."

"Now that's as far as I got with my research," Dan said. "There's a lot more to be said about surgery. You know, I was thinking, Mayo was born at the right time. He's specializing in surgery, and that's the profession of the future. But not for me! I'll stick to the internist work and the power of God in prayer. I guess I'm still part minister. Ambroise Paré once said, 'I dress his wounds, and God heals him!' That's my idea of a good doctor. I think there is a great future in the healing methods of Christ. The heart and the emotions must link hands with the medication, using all the natural help we can get."

Dan put down his papers. "Here I am doing all the talking, and you haven't said a word."

Etta shifted the leaves in her notebook. "Well, I took a spring slant," she answered. "I told you I felt spring in my bones! See how this sounds to you, Dan." Etta read:

"The pre-Lister period chills the bones. It was winter, snowed in with ignorance and superstition. The good things that came in the post-Pasteur period seemed to be hibernating, waiting for a good spring thaw.

"Then the sun shone through the fog." Etta went on, listing in detail the important scientific developments of the period.

"There is a medal for each medical hero who battled the stinging blasts of the bitter winters of the past," she concluded. "Tomorrow is a new day, yet there is work enough for all. We are in this army. We are coming into a heyday for the medical profession. As pioneers in the world of pain, we are the tools in God's hands to help this sick humanity which crowds our doors." Etta laid down her paper.

"It sounds like a good graduation address." Dan looked serious. "I was thinking, dear, I'll need a few clean shirts—and —would you know where our old suitcase is?"

"Daniel Kress! You didn't hear a word I read! You were thinking about a clean shirt and an old suitcase!" Etta looked hurt. "Just what do you want with your old suitcase?"

"Oh—I didn't tell you?" Dan looked sheepish. "Well, Dr. Kellogg has started a brand-new idea in Chicago."

8

"Chicago?" Etta gasped, open-mouthed.

Dan ignored her amazement. "Yes. It'll be a real mission field, and a great experience. He's opening a medical mission for the down-and-outers, they call them. When the World's Fair came to Chicago, a lot of men came for work. Of course some came with criminal intentions, too. But they all need help. Dr. Kellogg asked for volunteers——"

"And you volunteered!"

Dan nodded. "Three of us. I couldn't turn him down, Etta. Besides, it'll be good experience, and right in my field. I feel called to go. We can use the same method Jesus used to help people in His day, the physical combined with the spiritual. They must join hands as one."

Etta sat up straight. "Dan, I'm proud of you. Go, by all means. It will be a valuable experience. And do you know what I think?"

"What, dear?"

"I think that you're thirty years ahead of the world in your approach to your work. We're so fortunate to have our health message." She paused.

"Dan," Etta went on, "when we get through with our training and have our debts paid, I'd like to do something special." She was standing by Dan's chair, with a dreamy look on her face.

Dan looked up, surprised. "Yes?"

"Yes, I've been thinking. The girls are getting older now. We ought to—well, I suppose we should get our debt paid off first. Then, why couldn't we have a real home, and—have some more children?"

"Children? But—how could we afford——?"

Etta laughed. "I mean adopt some—a whole houseful! There are so many homeless waifs. Couldn't we, Dan?"

"I can't think of anything I would like any better, Mrs.

Kress. And it would be good for the girls, too. How about it if I put it down in my little black book?

"It would be nice to just live like people for a change, wouldn't it? But there are still several months before commencement. I must go down to Chicago for a little while. Meanwhile you work on your black silk, and Evelyn will work on her lavender and old lace." Dan laughed. "Etta, how about the clean shirts?" he added.

Etta finished, "And where is that old suitcase?"

* * * * *

My dearest Ones:

You can't imagine how I miss all of you tonight! It may not be a brave thing to be homesick—but I am, anyway!

You asked about the location of the mission, Etta. I can tell you without any exaggeration that it's in the worst part of the city. I'm glad it snowed last night, because it covered the worst of the dismal sight. Yet many people never see anything else.

We are near the Pacific Garden Mission, in fact. I've gotten acquainted with some of their directors. They're doing a fine work here in the slums, and there's plenty for all of us to do. I didn't realize before that this work was so new here in Chicago. The derelicts here wonder why men like us would come here to care for them.

Let me describe the place to you, Etta. We rent a basement and a street-level chapel. The basement was a dismal place until some light paint and bright curtains changed the atmosphere somewhat.

You can buy a good substantial meal here for three or four cents. Or if you don't have the three cents, we offer a large bowl of soup and zwieback free to those who have nothing—and I mean *nothing!*

First we give them a bath with plenty of soap and finish off with a good brisk hot and cold. The clothing goes into the disinfecting chamber, if it is wearable. If not, it goes into the furnace, and we furnish them with a decent outfit. We give some medical care and a free night's lodging with a clean bed and a clean nightshirt. That's not a bad service.

There's a continual lineup in the front hall. I can truthfully say I enjoy the work. I find a tender heart in most of these men. After the meals they are taken to the chapel, where we talk to them about Jesus. Many of them pray in earnest for the first time in their lives.

I've learned not to "call any man common or unclean." It's surprising, Etta, how a good hot and cold shower will sober up a drunk and almost make a man out of him.

Let me tell you about William. One evening I had finished my work for the day. I locked up the place and started to my room. I passed a poor fellow leaning against a railing in front of the saloon. His eyes were closed, and he could hardly keep on his feet. There was blood trickling down his face onto a filthy shirt.

I felt sorry for him, but I walked on by, excusing myself. I was tired. Hadn't I worked for these bums all day? So I walked on down the street.

About a block from the man I recalled vividly the story of the poor man from Jericho who had fallen among the thieves and been left for dead.

I went back. I put my hand on the fellow's shoulder and said, "If you'll come with me, I will get you cleaned up."

Without opening his eyes, he mumbled, "Who are you?"

"Never mind. I'm a friend. I want to help you."

Opening his bloodshot eyes, he muttered, "Too much kindness—too much kindness."

I took him by the arm and led him to the mission basement. I gave him a good bath with plenty of soap and a brisk hot and cold spray. He sobered right up. His clothes were filthy, so while he was shaving, I got him a clean outfit. The others went into the furnace.

After a prayer and a bowl of hot soup, he joined the group upstairs. Later I heard him give a sincere testimony that he was determined to live right. That night he prayed for the first time he could remember. I was so glad I had gone back.

I think, Etta, that the Lord has led me here. It's a good experience and has strengthened me spiritually. I wonder if all of our students should not have this help?

Hug our girls for me, dear. I miss all of you so much. Tell them about the notes I made in my little black book. You remember? It'll give them something good to look forward to. They will love sharing with someone else. I am looking forward to it myself, but for the present it must wait awhile.

You are always in my thought and prayers. I love you so much!

Your Dan

Chicago, Illinois
Spring is in the air—1894

My dear Etta:

I'm down by the parkway along the lake. The slums of Chicago are as repulsive to me as the whole world of sin must be to God.

I miss the green grass and the trees. Bryant used to say, "Go forth, under the open sky, and list to Nature's teachings." That suits me. Here I can listen to the waves as they break on the sand, and watch the greedy gulls wheeling about above the water looking for their food. It's very restful.

On the way here by trolley we crossed the new Chicago drainage canal. It's quite the project. They began this huge undertaking in 1892. It is 28 miles long and 160 feet wide. The purpose of it is to change the mouth of the Chicago

River (a thing never done before) and turn the sewage into a canal instead of letting it pollute Lake Michigan.

Chicago is right now the fastest-growing city in the country. Many people have flocked here for work. Of course, the city fathers are doing a wise thing to look ahead to see the need of a pure water supply for this huge metropolis. No wonder we at the mission are so busy. Many men are not finding work, and this creates our basic problem. They lounge around in the saloons, have a few drinks, then seek the houses of prostitution that are on many streets. It's so easy to drift into such a life. Etta, when I think of the things I have been spared, I thank God.

Oh, I must tell you about a lady I met here. She came to the mission for a bowl of soup. I noticed she had something in her lap wrapped in an old coat. I was curious, so I spoke to her. Her pitiful face was so thin. She looked half starved.

After her meal I took her into my office to hear her story. It was a sad one! Etta, the bundle wrapped in the old coat was a four-week-old baby. It had no clothes on! I was aghast.

We found some things for the baby, and I took her address. She said her husband was sick in bed.

The next day I called to see for myself. They lived in a dark room with no window or light from the outside. You just can't believe that people live as they do here. A candle burned by the bed where the husband lay. Was I surprised! This man was not a drunkard (as I had suspected), but an honest man, sick and discouraged. After I had helped them all I could, we had prayer together. While I was praying, I was strongly impressed to give him some money. I put my hand in my pocket, and when I got up, I gave him the last coin I had—a silver dollar. That dollar meant more to me than $100,000 would mean to Henry Ford!

Well, I've placed them in touch with our church welfare,

and they have provided for their needs. But guess what our folks told me. The dollar I gave those people kept them from being thrown out onto the street that night. Nothing less could really have helped them.

Who knows the good that can be done in a city like this, Etta? You and the girls pray for me. I want to be a faithful witness. Had I the choice to make again, I would still volunteer, even though I miss my family so much.

I love you all dearly—am starting to count the days until I can be home again. You will receive a box for you and the girls. I hope you will like it, dear. Now write often—and the girls, too. Even a short note is a real event in my day.

Always your lonely husband,
Daniel

Dearest:

Your letters give me a lift! You'll never know how much they mean to me here. I read them over and over. Thank Ora and Eva for their little notes. They're precious. Your letter was like a cool breeze on a hot day.

I hope you will never know what it is like to breathe the air of these slums. Even with spring again it is still awful. Some of these poor children never see anything clean and sweet and fresh. My heart aches for them. Every time I get a chance, I get a group of them together and tell them all I can about the lovely things in the world.

As you can guess, we have our problems here with drug addiction, as well as alcohol. I must tell you about one of them. This man heard of our work helping addicts. He was a physician and for more than twenty years has been using the hypodermic. He had formed this habit when he was in medical school.

As you know, Etta, we try to take away the drug immediately, but on the advice of his doctor, we agreed to cut down gradually, stating the amounts. After ten days' trial the patient was beside himself.

"Doctor," he cried to me, "I can't stand this any longer!"

"I am surprised you have stood it this long," I told him, assuring him that when he came to the place where he was willing to give it up and follow God's way, then God could help him.

With tears he finally said, "God help me, I will!"

We knelt there and prayed. It was surprising how easily he conquered. There are a number of cases—alcohol, tobacco, and dope—which could never have been conquered by diet alone or medical treatment alone. The more I see, the more I believe we must depend on God's help.

While I am on the subject, dear, let me tell you about another case. It haunted me. This fellow seemed so hopeless. In fact, he came to me to get me to sign an order for him to be admitted to the Washingtonian Home for Inebriates.

My heart went out to him. He was a well-educated man. I won't try to describe him, he seemed so pitiful. He was at the point of delirium tremens and wanted help badly, so I wrote the order for him.

Well, he came back later with a letter for me. When I opened and read it, this was the message: "He is a hopeless case. We can do nothing for him."

I could have wept. Instead, I told him that if he was really sincere, we could help him, and see what the Lord could do.

He smoked constantly. I said nothing about it for fear I would discourage the poor fellow by asking too much. Each day as I treated his sores, I prayed with him, and we studied the promises of the Bible. What do you suppose he asked me one day?

"Doctor, why don't you smoke?"

"I used to," I told him, "but I've found it defiles the body and the brain." I told him how it affects the heart and the capillaries by constricting the flow of blood and slowing down the circulation.

"With the sores you have," I told him, "you should give your body every chance to heal. But it will take a lot of good blood to do it."

He handed me his pipe and then his tobacco. "Take it; I am through with it!"

"Do you mean it?" I was surprised. "You'll have a time giving it up!"

He looked at me and smiled. "The Lord has given me victory over drink. He can do the same with tobacco!"

It was true. He had no difficulty giving it up either. He would smile and say, "Where sin abounded, grace did much more abound."

He left and went home. Now I have a letter. You should see his beautiful handwriting. He asked me here about the Sabbath. I never even mentioned the subject to him. So I have his letter now to answer. Someday, Etta, we'll walk the streets of gold with that man, for he is a true overcomer. His name is John Ferren.

This has turned out to be quite a long letter, but I like to tell you when these things are fresh on my mind.

I'm counting the days until I come home. I'll be the happiest man on that train. It will be heaven to be home again with you and the girls, but all my life I think I'll be glad I came to this place. I guess half my heart will always be here in the slums with these men that I've learned to love.

Have the girls count down the hours for us. Hug them tight for me. I love you always.

Dan

"Cheaper by the Dozen"

*T*HE DOCTOR is not in! Say it, Dickie Boy!" It was the cheery voice of six-year-old Ora coaxing the parrot.

Dickie tipped his colorful head this way and that. "Dickie wanta cracker—a fruit cracker," he said plainly.

Ora coaxed some more. "If you'll say, 'The doctor is not in,' then I'll get you a fruit cracker."

But the bird would not cooperate.

Just then the door opened, and there was the doctor. "Hello, Doc," Dickie welcomed him. "Good-bye now," he added gaily, trying to attract attention.

Dr. Kress and Ora laughed as they gave him his tidbit. Turning to her father, Ora threw her arms around his neck. He carried her to the nearest rocker and deposited her on his lap.

"Papa, I've been thinking."

"Oh?"

"About that little black book and the promise you wrote down once. Remember?"

"I believe I do. Let's see; it must still be——"

"It's in your pocket—that one."

The doctor fished until he found it. "Here it is, Sugar," he said, handing it to her. "Now—what was it you wanted to see?"

Ora quickly turned the pages. "Right there. Read that to me. You promised that when we finished our medical courses ——"

"Oh, yes. And we have now finished our—yes, we have, haven't we?" Then he read, " 'I promise to get a larger house and have a large family when we are through with our medical courses.' "

Ora put in quickly, "And this is the big house, so now can't we have our family? I want a baby brother." Ora cuddled in her father's lap.

"Of course you do, Ora. And this house needs a few more children. But you girls would have to help with the housework, and you wouldn't get as many dresses."

"Oh, that wouldn't matter. We need someone else to play with."

Ora was right. The big house on Barbour Street needed to embrace a big family, to have children's voices laughing and singing and even crying. That was why, when the doctors had graduated, they chose this house. It could shelter all the frets and fusses, all the love and laughter, the teen-age tempests and the teething tantrums. In fact, that's what big houses are for.

The Kresses graduated in May, 1894. Dr. Lauretta had worn her new black silk with a touch of lace, and Evelyn, the classic classmate, had promenaded in her lavender gown with the flowing train. The diplomas now hung, neatly framed, side by side in the hallway. Battle Creek had become their home, and here they had found the big house with the wide-open arms.

But now it was Christmastime. Two not-so-small girls were carried down the long flight of stairs by their parents. Their long flannel nightgowns almost covered their feet. Laughing and squirming, they scrambled toward the gaily decorated Christmas tree in the big living room.

"Merry Christmas, girls!"

"Oh—Mamma—Papa! Look, Eva!" Four big eyes widened. Two girls, awed by their gifts, knelt by a small crib to see a real doll, laughing and playing with his toes. Pinned to his pillow was a note: "To Eva and Ora. Here is your little brother, Paul. We've kept our promise in the little black book. Happy Christmas! Mamma and Papa."

The popcorn loops that hung on the fragrant tree seemed to dance with delight. The strings of red cranberries glistened as if they had been varnished. This Christmas was full of laughter and happiness, with three children instead of two. But what would happen by next Christmas?

The next Christmas was a living fairy tale. The house reverberated with the laughter of many children. There was dark-eyed Anna, a young lady of fourteen. There was Alice, age twelve. They were such sweet girls that when another girl turned up by the name of Sylvia, the Kresses decided to keep her, too. Sylvia was not wanted at home, nor was her young brother, Frank. Their mother worked all the time, and Frank was getting to be a neglected little street ruffian. Dr. Lauretta's heart went out to him. "Why not take him, too?" she wondered. Perhaps she could find a home for him nearby.

When Dr. Dan saw the mischievous dimple and the sweet smile with which Frank was blessed, he couldn't resist. "Etta, we still need another boy now to play with Frank," he suggested.

"But, Dan, I thought we'd just keep Sylvia."

"Now, Mother, must we have all girls in this house? I say No, we need some boys, too!"

And Dan had his way. Furthermore, it was not long before the news of the adoptions got around. Anthony and Charles and Lois joined the family, but they were mere babies.

The governess was the manager when the Kresses were away at their offices each day. They all managed so well that when a bachelor patient asked if they would take his two nephews—guess what happened?

William was twelve and was tall for his age, and Theodore was fifteen. Once they were orphans, but not now!

The big white house was bulging. The last venture was
Allen, whose father died at the sanitarium. Allen was thirteen,
and a lot of fun. The big boys and girls managed nicely together as a rule. But rules sometimes caused problems.

"Mother, come here. Frankie swore some bad words." Willie
dragged Frank into the house by the collar of his shirt.

Lauretta, unperturbed, looked Frank in the eye without
saying a word. Then she calmly said, "Let me see inside
your mouth."

Frank opened it wide.

"What a dirty mouth you have! The idea! You know what
we do when your hands are dirty, Frank."

Walking him to the washbasin as she talked, she took the
nailbrush, washed it thoroughly, then scrubbed the boy's
tongue until his mouth was full of lather.

"Now do you think that will clean out those dirty words?"

Frank nodded as the tears ran down his cheeks.

"We don't talk that way here, Frank. I hope I don't have to
do this again."

Frank needed some new clothes, and so did the other
children. "Sorry, not for a while," Dr. Dan explained. "The
bank account is too low."

Then the mailman came. There was a letter. The writer of
this letter knew about the big houseful of children. A twenty-
dollar check was enclosed. Wonderful! What could Etta do
with twenty dollars? The house rang with the happy news.
Frank got his needs fulfilled, and so did some of the others.
When the clothes were handed out that night, there was a real
surprise for the whole family.

"While everyone is in a good mood, we decided to have a
party. Girls——" Dr. Dan looked about.

In walked the girls with a bouquet of fragrant red roses,
tagged "For Mother."

"It was the girls' idea, Etta. They put me up to it. You know I can never remember birthdays."

"You'll have no excuse now with all these girls to help you." Etta laughed. There was a birthday cake with candles, and popcorn balls for everyone.

Dan stood up. "While you're all munching so quietly on your popcorn balls," he said, "I want to tell you children a few things about your mother here. You girls can take notes, for it won't be too long before some fine young man will be coming around here wondering what kind of girl you are. What can I tell them? And you big boys—you're beginning to notice what makes a good wife. Well, I can tell you.

"You all know it is hard for me to keep money in my pockets." Dan chuckled. "You ought to see how your mother does it. She's a good manager. She knows where her money goes. She even demands that I tell her where mine goes. 'Now —what did you pay out today?' she asks, and before you know it, she has it all down in the little black book.

"Your mother never leaves a debt unpaid. In fact, I think she loves to pay them off.

"Another thing, children, no matter how busy she is, your mother remembers all the birthdays—am I right?"

The noise that followed was hard on the ears, but dad was right. Birthdays were important, and they all knew it.

"You boys, now. If you can find a wife like your mother, then I won't worry about your being happy. Make up your mind to have a neat Christian home, and God will bless you. All of you that love your mother join me in singing 'Happy Birthday to You.' "

Henry Ward Beecher once said, "I love the smell of Chinese honeysuckle. A man does not need to see it to know that it is in bloom."

So it was in the big house on the hill. One knew there was

honeysuckle there, for the sweet, overpowering fragrance of Christian love filled every room to overflowing.

* * * * *

Spring came again to Battle Creek, Michigan. The door of winter stood ajar. The icicles melted drip by drip, then fell like brave soldiers giving up the battle.

On the lawn the Kress children romped and played. Some of them had taken off their long black stockings and their high-topped shoes. But Eva was missing.

Upstairs the Doctors Kress softly closed the door of Eva's room and stepped quietly into the hallway.

"What do you make of it, Mother?" Dan asked.

"It must be endocarditis again. She's running the same fever."

"How do you feel about our call to England?" Dan's face was sober. His eyes looked tired and anxious.

"Well, let's pray about it some more, Dan. I was glad for the call. Lecturing is your field, and editing the health journal should be an interesting job. I think God needs us to start the work in England. They say there's no one else qualified to go. But what do we do with the children now? How can we give them up after all the fun we've had with them?"

"And selling the house," Dan added. "I've been praying that God would lead us, but with Eva sick again——"

"Papa, Mamma—come here, will you?" The voice came from Eva's room. Quickly the doctors went in to their daughter.

"Papa, maybe I wasn't supposed to hear, but I did. I'm fourteen now, and I think I understand how you feel. May I say something?" Eva reached out to take her father's hand.

"Why not?" The doctor stroked Eva's small hand.

"I've been praying too, and what I think is—if God opens a door for us, shouldn't it be a sign for us to walk through it?" Dan and Etta nodded questioningly.

"Then I think we should try to find good homes for the children," Eva declared. "There are many good Christian homes right around here. Then we can sell the furniture and the house.

"Besides, about my being sick, God can make me well if He wants to, and He knows what's best. I'm not afraid to die. He can raise me from the dead as easily as He could make me in the first place! Can't He, Papa?"

Dan bent down to kiss his daughter's hot forehead. There were tears in his eyes. "Yes, of course, Eva, of course."

Etta sat down carefully on the bed beside her sick daughter. "I think you've been very mature in your reasoning, Eva. God bless you, dear."

Dan straightened her pillow before they left. He was amazed that the wisdom of a child would guide them on through the turbulent days ahead. It was a difficult time for all of them. The children were reluctant to go to new homes. They had been with the Kresses for nearly five years. Lauretta and Dan decided that only Paul should stay. They made plans for the others, and sad good-byes were said. The furniture was finally all sold, and the date for the sailing was set for Monday, April 2, 1899.

There had not been one buyer for the house until the day before the Kresses were supposed to leave. Every room was bare and clean. Etta was finishing the tedious process of packing the trunks when the front doorbell rang insistently. It echoed like an alarm through the empty house.

The gentleman at the door said simply, "I understand this house is for sale."

"Why—why, yes, sir, it is. Come in, please!" Etta showed him not only the house, but the barn, the buggy, the horse, and the cow. He seemed pleased with the place and the price.

"Now"—he smiled pleasantly—"if my wife likes it, we're all set!"

9

And she did like it!

"There's only one catch," Lauretta explained. "We are leaving for my parents' place in Detroit at two o'clock tomorrow. Then we go on to England."

"To England!" The man caught his breath. "My, my!"

That evening the farewell reception was given for the Kresses at the Battle Creek Sanitarium parlor. Right in the middle of the festivities the new buyer appeared, asking to speak to Daniel a minute.

"I'm sorry to break in on your party, Doctor, but it's urgent. Could you folks meet us at the bank at ten o'clock tomorrow morning?"

"We'll be glad to, sir."

"We'll have the money for you then." The man seemed relieved.

"Well, yes, certainly. May I add that you folks have been an answer to our prayers?" Dan was as happy as a boy with a new toy. He shook the man's hand warmly, and his face beamed as he related the experience to his friends.

"Now I know, and so do all of you, that God is leading us in this venture. I thought you should hear it from us."

Unfortunately, Eva seemed to get worse in the next few days. Her fever went higher. Being anxious about her, the family stayed in Detroit as long as they could.

Again little doubts nipped at Daniel's heels. Again he walked slowly to Eva's room to gain assurance, for if Dan would admit it or not, this girl gave him courage to forge ahead.

"Eva, my girl, you look better today." Dan patted her hand.

"I am, Papa. Look. I've been drawing boats. Will our big boat look like this one, or this one?"

"Probably neither one. I'm sorry to disappoint you, but— here, give me your pencil. Ocean liners are huge things, like this, dear."

"That big? Where do we sleep?"

"Here!"

"I was lying here wondering—does everyone get seasick, Papa?"

The question gave Dan a start. Why hadn't he thought of that? Would it be safe for Eva? Then he laughed.

"I was thinking, Eva, how awkward it would be if all the crew on a boat got sick. Then who would take care of me when I got sick? No, honey, some do and some don't."

"And we won't because God can help us, can't He? He helped us sell the cow and the horse and the house the very last day, so we won't worry about seasickness."

"Eva, you always do me a lot of good." Dan kissed Eva's warm cheek. "None of us realize how much influence we have on other people, do we? It's full speed ahead for the Kress family!"

"Aye, aye, Captain!" Eva saluted, her sweet smile brightening the room and sending a ray of hope into the wind-tossed future.

"Oh, to Be in England"

*L*ONDON in 1899 was a quaint old city, drenched in the perfume of lilacs, framed with rambling roses. Fences were embroidered with them like lace on an old-fashioned dress; old houses hid gratefully behind their beauty. Old walls, bowed with the years, spread out their arms to encircle them.

Children, happy to be emancipated from the clutches of winter, played "London Bridge Is Falling Down," but London, proud of its famous bridge, actually kept it in good repair.

London, aware that an era was ending, seemed determined to make an impression on this age. A gay, almost daring trend in feminine fashion appeared. To the long, street-sweeping dress already in vogue was added the wasp waist. The huge gathered balloon sleeve and the wide-brimmed, lavishly decorated hats made many a man gaze in wonder at what was coming down the street. The girls accomplished their aim. Eventually the world turned its head to look.

Swaggering swains now carried walking sticks, a sort of fancy miniature cane which gave a new dignity to their bearing. The goatee and the beard were still worn, but the goatee was definitely more popular.

London, then as now, was not made up solely of swaggering swains or fashion-conscious females, but of ordinary people with large families who worked hard for every cent. Each family had its own unique problem. The Kress family was no exception. To be suddenly set down on the shores of a new country was thrilling. At the same time to be heralded as the doctors from Battle Creek Sanitarium was a huge responsibility, for the American institution was world famous, and many wealthy people had already been there, seeking to regain their lost health.

Etta's daytime was taken up with cooking classes and lectures. The big thing in Dan's life was the new health journal for which he was responsible. But the evenings were the most exciting. To see a huge hall filled with people willing and eager to learn about a more healthful way of living was most rewarding.

"Can you help me, dear?" Dan called to his small wife at home one evening. "I've been trying all day to line up these articles for this first issue of the London *Life and Health*. Look, Etta."

Etta looked. Dan had spread out all his material on the living-room carpet.

"I think I'll aim to have something for each age of the family. I want the children and the young people to have something, too. Look. If I do a question column for the boys, will you do one for the girls? I think they'll be more apt to read it if it's questions. This time I'll have to make up the questions myself. Here, see what these sound like." Dan turned to his wife. "Etta, you aren't listening! Why don't you answer?"

"Dan, I've never seen you so wrapped up in anything before —not like this."

"I thought you weren't interested."

"Interested! I'm thrilled! You enjoy it, don't you? Certainly I'll do your girls' column."

Dan smiled. "Of course I enjoy it."

"Here's an idea," Etta added. "Get some of the prominent doctors here to write articles for you, or why not interview patients who have been to Battle Creek, or——"

Dan held up his hand. "Wait—I thought you weren't interested. I was wondering what I would put in the next issue. I had begun to think I put all I knew in this one!" Dan laughed. "Cheerio, as they say here. I think we'll make it. Being an editor isn't such a bad job after all."

But being an editor was only one of Dan's jobs. One day a conference president called at his downtown office. The gentleman seemed highly elated. He shook the doctor's hand with much enthusiasm.

"Well, Dr. Kress, I've found it!" His eyes sparkled. His face beamed.

"Good, good!" exclaimed Dan, laughing. "Now, would you mind telling me just what you have found?"

"That I will. Sorry I was so precipitate. But I have been eager to locate a place for our London sanitarium, and I really believe I've found it. In fact, I actually made a deposit on the place to hold it. Now would you and Dr. Lauretta go over at your earliest convenience and give us your O.K.? We want to get this thing started soon. We'll get you folk in the harness yet!"

Dan smiled. "We feel as though we are already in the harness. In fact, we like our harness pretty well. The lecturing, and the cooking school, and this journal here. The first issue is ready for the press." Dan looked proud.

"Good, good! And we appreciate what you folk are doing. Did you see the article in the paper about your experiences in the Chicago slums? This antitobacco, antiliquor idea you have is a new one for London. The whole town is talking about it. God will work for us here. By the way, Doctor, the committee meets on Wednesday evening about that building for the new sanitarium. We'll see you there."

The report to the committee on Wednesday night was a different thing. The whole enthusiastic group was utterly disappointed, because the location for the new sanitarium was totally unsuitable. To reach it one had to go through the worst part of London, which was at best not much better than the slums of Chicago.

Dr. Kress suggested that the work they might do for the down-and-outers of London would have to wait awhile. The buildings would not house the patients or the workers comfortably. The grounds were nonexistent. The whole committee voted against the purchase, and the deposit was lost.

About this time the doldrums took over. The wind in everybody's sails vanished. A few weeks later a letter was received at the conference office from the dedicated pen of Ellen White. She gave this advice: "The new London sanitarium should be located at least twenty miles from London, where the air would not be contaminated with smoke and dust."

God did lead. Another place was found. It was at "Dunedin," Meadvale, Surrey Hills. This property met all the requirements. It had been a women's college. The grounds were spacious and well landscaped; the shrubs and flowers were lovely. There was a tennis court, a croquet court, a flower and vegetable garden. There were plenty of rooms for both the patients and the employees.

"This is the place!" was everyone's opinion.

Then wonderful things happened. A generous gentleman wrote to Daniel. He had heard and believed the doctor's lectures.

"I'm giving up my large home," he said. "I want to ship all my furnishings to help in furnishing the new sanitarium."

With great joy the gift was accepted. Imagine the lovely drapes, carpets, bedding, glassware, china, pictures, and furniture of every kind. There was even a piano, a real luxury.

Now there was wind in every sail. The employees organized to get the place ready for the grand opening. It was an ambitious undertaking. Imagine uniforming and organizing a new class of nurses, besides all the other things which must be done. Well-to-do people, eager to have in London a place like the Battle Creek establishment, gave their help and wished the Kresses much success.

The big day was September 2, 1899. In a wheelchair pushed by her sister, Ora, Eva toured the lovely grounds. How they enjoyed the flowers and the spacious campus! It was a big day for everyone. Now the cooking and the health classes could be conducted at the sanitarium. Lectures were also given there for the patients.

A few weeks later Etta chanced to find Dan napping in his rocker. "He looks tired," she thought. "Perhaps it's just all the commotion of late, but he looks utterly exhausted."

"Mamma!" Ora came bouncing into the room.

"Sh-sh! You'll wake your father."

Ora began to whisper. "Mamma, I thought I should tell you, Eva's sick again. She said not to tell, but I thought you ought——"

Dan roused. "Eva sick? Where is she, Ora?"

"She's in her room, Papa. I'm sorry if I woke you."

"That's all right, honey. Let's go see her."

Ora skipped along with her father's hand in hers. "She's hot on her head again, Papa."

"Papa!" Eva cried, holding out her hands. "I told her not to tell."

"Then how could we help you, dear? Ora did the right thing. I'm so sorry you're feeling worse again. I was hoping it was all over."

"Papa, I—I feel so tired this time. Why should I feel so tired?"

"My girl, this time I'm calling a heart specialist. This thing has gone too far already."

The heart specialist came and prescribed treatment, but the fever still persisted. Eva suffered very little pain, but each day she seemed to weaken.

"I'm going to pull the steamer chair right by your bed, Eva," Etta told her. "I'll be right here if you want me. Just reach out and touch me, dear."

"But, Mamma, you need your rest. You've worked all day. I'll be all right."

"Look! I brought you a surprise."

"Where did you ever get oranges?" Eva was excited.

"Special treat for a sick girl. We love you, dear."

"It tastes wonderful." Then suddenly her smile faded a little. "Mamma, does it hurt when you die?"

Lauretta gulped and swallowed hard. She was always truthful. She answered slowly, "Sometimes, dear."

"Mamma, I want you to know I'm not afraid to die." Eva's eyes were big. Her voice was brave for a fifteen-year-old. "It's wonderful to know we will be resurrected. I was reading about Lazarus today. Mamma, are you listening? Now don't cry. If I'm not afraid, then you shouldn't be. Ora, Ora, you come here, too. I want you to know I'm not afraid to die!"

"But, Eva, you got better before," Etta encouraged.

"When Jesus comes, He'll wake me up just as He did Lazarus."

Etta interrupted, "Eva, dear, don't talk that way!"

Ora kissed her sister good-night, and as she waved to her from the doorway, Eva said, "See you in the morning."

Eva's words echoed uneasily in Lauretta's ears. She couldn't sleep, even though her sick daughter was sleeping soundly beside her.

"In the morning," she thought. "O God, how can we give her up? Must we give her up now in the bloom of her life, now when she means so——"

A whisper came from the doorway. "Etta?" It was Dan.
"Dan, I can't give her up! I can't, I can't——"
"Sweetheart, she may still get better."
"No, she's weaker every day. O Dan——"
"You're too tired, Etta. Let me sit with her tonight. You
get undressed and go to bed—doctor's orders!" Gently Dan
laid back the covers and tucked his tired wife under the soft
blanket, kissing her tenderly. Then sliding to the edge of the
bed, with his hand still in hers, he poured out his heart to the
God they both loved.

He stooped to say good-night. "Sleep, darling. You'll feel
better in the morning. I love you for all you've done." Then he
was gone, and the door closed softly behind him.

Nights and days of vigil melted together in memory. September passed into October. One week, two weeks——

"See you in the morning, that bright morning," Eva whispered weakly. "Papa, I'm not afraid to die——"

"I know, dear."

"Don't cry, Papa."

Eva said no more. She gasped a little as Dan wiped his
eyes. He turned quickly and stooped over his daughter.

"Eva! Eva!" Dan grasped her wrist. There was no pulse.
Then Dan called, "Etta, Etta, come here! O Etta, she's gone!
Eva's gone!"

Ora followed closely at her mother's heels. "O Mamma! We
didn't even get to say good-bye to her. She always said to me,
'See you in the morning.' Now she's gone!"

Eva died on October 16, 1899. For weeks the Kresses
seemed to be in a daze, stunned and weeping. The loss was
staggering, almost unbelievable. Rejecting reality, they visited
her grave. They walked into her room, half forgetting that she
wasn't there. In a fog they sat in church, resigned, yet stunned.
Ora clung to the words she would always remember—"See you

in the morning." They became a cherished thread that strung together the bits of life which must go on.

But Daniel was not the same. Etta scrutinized him as he napped in his favorite chair. Again she thought, "He seems so utterly exhausted. His color is bad. What can be wrong with my Dan?"

Dan awoke with a start. "Oh, was I asleep again? My, but I feel tired to the bone tonight. Think I'll go right to bed, dear. You better come, too. We are both too tired since Eva died."

"Dan, I wish you'd get a good checkup. You look pale to me."

"Pale? Oh, I'll feel better in the morning." Memories again! How they haunted him at every turn. Dan kissed his wife, knowing she understood.

The night was much like any other, but the morning was a different story.

"Etta, something's wrong with me—look, I can't get up! I—I feel—all gone. Help me, dear!"

Dr. Lauretta Kress evaluated the situation quickly.

"You stay right in bed. I'm calling the doctor."

The doctor came and immediately advised complete rest and a warmer climate for Dan.

How could Dan be happy, even in the relaxing warmth of southern France? He obeyed the doctor, yet to think of Lauretta enduring the damp, cold winter in London was almost unthinkable. The burden of managing the sanitarium was left for her small shoulders.

The patients came and went; the nurses had their training; the work went on. The long winter was finally ended. "Oh, to be in England, now that April's there," became Dan's theme song, borrowed from Robert Browning.

But April finally came, and Dan came home to London and his family. He looked much better.

"You can't imagine how wonderful it is just to be home," he said with a smile.

"And you can't imagine how wonderful it is just to have you home again," Etta replied.

"I'm going down to the office, Etta."

"All right, but I have an appointment for you with your doctor. He wants to check you over. Ten o'clock, Dan."

A few days passed. Etta found the report as she was opening the mail. It was frightening! Pernicious anemia! How could that be? Etta frowned as she read the report again. Why, anemia was a fatal disease! Despair threw its mantle of gloom about Etta's shoulders.

A bit overwrought, Etta quickly jotted a letter to their family friend Dr. Kellogg. Before Dan came home, she had mailed it.

Back in the house again, she wondered. Should she tell Dan about the report? Would it make him discouraged and depressed? Surely he would know there was no cure for pernicious anemia. Tears long overdue fell upon the laboratory report, splashing softly on the paper.

Then the Niagara broke loose. Etta, the brave one, now flung herself onto a kitchen chair and was convulsed with sobs. She buried her face in her hands. Why did these things have to happen to them? Were they not here doing their best for God? Had He turned His face away from them? Would she even now lose that one person in this world she needed most? She didn't hear the quiet footsteps of her husband as he came in the door.

"Darling, Etta, what's wrong?" Dan's warm arms were about her.

"Dan, why does everything have to happen to us?" More sobs.

"We mustn't be discouraged, Etta. It's a tool of Satan. Look at me, dear." Dan chuckled as he juggled Etta's chin in his hand. "You're too tired. You have had all the responsibilities too long. Now that I'm home, it's my turn to take things in hand. Will you relax now?"

"Dan"—Etta decided to tell him—"here's the report." The tears started to fall again. "Why—why should you have pernicious anemia?"

Dan sat down wearily. It was like a knife stabbing into him. Dan, the lecturer, the doctor, the editor of a health magazine. Dan the teacher of others! How could this happen to him?

"Dan, I'm sorry I was such a crybaby. I don't cry very often. Do you have a clean hanky?"

Reaching into his back pocket, Dan produced a neatly folded handkerchief. Etta blew her nose properly. Then she said, "I want to tell you I just now mailed a letter to Dr. Kellogg."

"Kellogg?"

"Dan, I can't lose you, too." Etta threw her arms around her husband. "O sweetheart!" The intonation was meaningful.

Dan patted her arm which clung to him. Then thoughtfully he said, "I don't understand. How could it be anemia? I've tried so hard to eat right, to live right, to be the right example."

"Could you get the right foods last winter? I wondered about that."

"It was hard. Everyone tried hard to make delicious desserts and rich, greasy gravies. There was grease in everything, and it was repulsive to me. I tried to get fruit, and I was trying to do without eggs and milk."

Etta looked surprised. All she said was, "Do you think that's wise at this time? Maybe I better start to feed you right." She smiled for the first time.

Dan looked up in time to catch it. "I like your smile," he said simply. "Let's pray about it. Shall we kneel right here?"

Dr. Kellogg's cable came as a shock. It read, "Have good courage. Can help him. Daniel to sail to U.S. Live with me. Dr. J. H. Kellogg."

He sailed on June 14. There were tears and smiles, and the waving of big white handkerchiefs from the deck of the ocean liner. Good-byes again—how Etta began to despise the word! She stood there on the dock watching the boat move slowly away from her. Dan was still barely in sight, still waving his big handkerchief. The questions circled, widening, widening. Would they ever see Dan again? Turning to Ora, Etta sighed deeply. Ora was sobbing softly.

"Mamma, we have each other, and the doctor says he can help papa. I guess that's all that really matters. When the other doctors come here, then we can go home, can't we?"

"You darling girl! Ora, you're braver than I am. I tell you what. When I'm blue, you cheer me; and when you're blue, I'll cheer you."

"All right, Mamma. I'm glad I have you."

Back at the sanitarium they were busy enough. One day the new doctors finally arrived. Dr. Olsen and his wife were good help. Lauretta's lagging spirits revived, and the long summer finally passed on dragging feet.

Then the cable came. Good news. "You are to leave on the *Laurentian* from Glasgow, Scotland, September 6, 1900."

With mixed emotions Etta left. Good-byes again circled the blue waters, but this time she was the one who was waving the big white handkerchief to her friends on the pier. There were tears again, for hearts in London town are warm even if their weather is cold.

The *Laurentian* was an old boat, and the off-coast waters were foggy and rough. That night the darkness settled about them as the old boat pitched and tossed. Ora cuddled close to her mother and was soon sound asleep, but for Etta sleep would not come. Seasick and frightened, she listened to the creaking of every board as the boat groaned its way through the rough seas. She prayed for the morning. Would it never come? Thoughts of gloom must be replaced by thoughts of trust. Why not count all the blessings?

So there in the darkness, with her child warm and trusting near her, Lauretta began.

"Well, we got the *Life and Health* journal started, and it will go on to be a blessing to London. That's one pebble tossed into the water. Let's see. The sanitarium now has a good footing. Dr. Olsen and his wife are dedicated people. They'll carry on. The nurses' class will be a help even before they are through with their training. Then there were the lectures, but God can take all these pebbles and cast them into the sea of people, and He can widen their influences to be something big, something that England can build on.

"What does the Lord have ahead for us? O God, I feel like this old boat, adrift and unanchored in the rough waters of life."

With a prayer on her lips and dawn creeping over a restless ocean, Etta dropped off to sleep. Surely He who guides His children will bring them to their desired haven.

The Land "Down Under"

DR. DANIEL KRESS folded the letter carefully.

"Who's it from, Papa?"

"Another call, Ora. They need help now in the Land of the Kangaroo."

Ora, now twelve, laughed gaily. "And how could we help a kangaroo? You mean Australia? I'd like that; wouldn't you?"

Dan's blue eyes twinkled. "Wonder what your mother would think about it?"

Ora wondered too, but not for long. She skipped into the kitchen.

"Mamma, what do you know about kangaroos?"

"Very little, Ora." Etta went on kneading the whole-wheat bread as though she enjoyed it. Looking interested, Ora washed her hands and asked, "May I make some rolls?"

Etta nodded. "Here's a pan. Grease it good. The oil is there in the cabinet. Whatever were you and your father so worked up about?"

"Kangaroos and koala bears."

"Ora——"

"That's right, Mamma. We have an invitation to come to Australia. I think we ought to go. They need us."

"But your father's not well, Ora."

"Maybe it would help him get well quicker. It's a tropical place. There would be sunshine and fresh air and all kinds of

fruit. And we could stop at Pitcairn, and Honolulu, and——
How far is it?"

Lauretta laughed. "Is what? Suppose you give us a report
on it after supper tonight."

All afternoon the questions played hide and seek with each
other in the minds of the Kresses. As always the cloud of Dan's
illness hung over them, for anemia was still almost a stranger
in the medical world. It seemed to elude the friendly overtures
of the doctors. The trouble usually began with a pale appearance of the skin and a feeling of exhaustion. The appetite was
feeble, and the stomach failed to produce any secretions to di-
gest the food. The bone marrow failed to make red cells. In
those days the accepted treatment was hydrochloric acid to aid
digestion and arsenic to stimulate the bone marrow. Blood
transfusions were also given. The patient might live as long as
four years.

"Papa, look!" Ora searched in her pocket. Warm and cuddly
in her long flannelette nightgown, she snuggled in her father's
arms as he rested in his favorite rocker. "I'm glad you're feeling
better, Papa. It was awfully lonely in England without you."
Ora was a chatterbox, and Dan liked that. "Look what I did
today." Out of her pocket she pulled a neatly folded paper.
"Guess what?"

"You tell me, Ora. I'm not much good at guessing any
more."

"A koala bear is a marsupial. It has a pouch like a kangaroo. I'd like to have a koala bear, Papa."

"My dear girl, we have enough mouths to feed. I suppose
you'd want a kangaroo, too."

By this time Ora was laughing. "Papa, you surprise me with
your ignorance. A koala bear wouldn't cost a cent to feed—he
eats eucalyptus leaves."

"Well, I deserved that one, I guess. Mother, come here,

will you? Ora is about to give us an exposé of her findings. Have a chair and listen."

Etta obeyed silently.

The lid was off the chatterbox. Ora babbled on. "We go by train to the West Coast. We take an ocean liner to Honolulu. They put flowered leis around our necks. And I think we should stay there a month because of papa, as Dr. Kellogg advised. Then we go on to Pitcairn. I want to stay there a few days, too. Don't you, Papa?"

"Yes, very much," replied Dan. "Your mother will, too."

Ora went on. "Now we go to the land 'down under.' This continent used to be called New Holland. I didn't know that before. Did you, Mamma?"

Etta shook her head.

"It's as large as the United States, and the whole continent is really an island. We glide into the world's loveliest harbor, Sydney. The bridges drape across the water like steel lace."

Etta and Dan laughed.

"And they raise sheep there by the acre. I mean—what would you say, acres of them, or miles of them? But here's what you want to know. They have almost every kind of fruit you could think of. It's a tropical paradise. And wells are just like fountains. They run and run."

"You mean artesian? You've got a lot of information there, Ora."

"Wait till you hear about the kangaroo. It's incredible——"

"Watch out for that big word. You're likely to trip."

"I love nice big words, Mamma. Did you ever hear that people eat kangaroo? That is, the aborig—Papa, help me!"

"Aborigines, the natives," Daniel said.

"You're a smart man, Papa. Did you know that kangaroo-tail soup is a favorite with the abor—the natives? I found out a lot about kangaroos that I thought you ought to know."

Dan cleared his throat, and Etta managed a smile.

Ora went on: "There are fifty kinds. Some are small like a rat. They live in trees. Some, the big boomers they are called, are seven feet tall, and they can jump twenty feet in one jump. I didn't know before that they eat grass like a sheep. Guess what their enemies are. Eagles, wild dogs, and the python."

"Python! I didn't know Australia had pythons." This from Dan.

"Well, it does." Ora continued: "This was cute about the mother kangaroo. If she's attacked by a dingo—that's a wild dog—and she's carrying her little joey—that's the baby—in her pouch, she runs near a thick bush and throws the baby into the bush. Then she can run better, and if she's caught, the baby is safe.

"Then the mother leads the wild dog to the water. She runs into the water herself, catches the dog, and holds him under until he stops struggling. Then she goes back, picks up her baby, and goes on her way."

"How clever!" Etta exclaimed.

Dan got up and started pacing the floor. "What I'm most interested in is the new sanitarium being built in Sydney. Perhaps the Lord does want us there."

Did God really want them to pioneer the work in Sydney? It was made a matter of special prayer by the whole family. Secretly Dan prayed for a specific indication to direct him.

Dan had another blood test scheduled for the next week. The last test had been disappointing. The red count had been 1,250,000, and the normal count should have been four times that amount.

The tests were taken. When Dr. Frank Otis saw the results, he shook his head. "There must be some mistake here," he muttered to himself.

Later in the day when he saw Dan, he said, "There must be

a mistake made somewhere on your count, Doctor. Would you like to have me take it over?" Dr. Otis handed the report to Dan, an anxious look on his face.

Dan's face beamed like the sun coming from behind a dark cloud. The count was almost normal. "No, Frank, I don't think there was a mistake. You know we've had a call to go to Australia? Well, I asked God to give me a sign. This is it." Dan handed the report back to the laboratory technician. "God has been good to spare me. I want to go wherever He leads me. Thank you, Frank. I'm a happy man."

On October 13, 1900, the Kresses boarded the train for the West Coast. They were the only passengers in their sleeper. For five days they enjoyed the beautiful scenery that rushed by their window. God seemed eager to prove His love for these willing workers.

"You're my special charges—royalty," the porter said, smiling. "This stove here can be used for cooking if you like. You may fix your meals right here. Let me help in any way. That's my job. By the way, there are forty passengers in the next coach."

"I feel like royalty," Dan remarked to Etta. "We have seen God's hand on the circumstances of our lives, but this is a special."

"And we appreciate it," Etta added gratefully.

* * * * *

Honolulu was the first stop made by their boat, the *Auranzi*. As Ora and Dr. Kellogg had suggested, they would all have loved to stay in that island paradise.

But why did Daniel and Etta, each in their own minds, decide that they should go on with the boat?

"I've been impressed that we shouldn't stay," Dan declared. "I don't know why."

"But, Papa, we were going to stay here a month! Don't

you remember?" Ora begged, "It's perfect here. Look at the sunshine, the delicious fruit. Papa, can't we stay?"

"I'm sorry, my dear, but when God leads, we must let Him lead. Your mother and I both have a feeling we should go. There must be a reason."

Consequently the Kress family arrived in the world's most beautiful harbor a month earlier than they had planned. A hurried telegram brought someone to meet them.

"Welcome to our country!" The friendly Australian shook the hands of the Americans. "You're just in time. The council of doctors for this area is meeting tomorrow. They will want all of your credentials, diplomas, and your credits. Usually these are presented two weeks in advance of this meeting, but we'll just take them with us. I'm sure they will make a concession."

The next few weeks were occupied with house hunting. A nice house, still under construction, was found for the Kresses. But Dan was worried. The next medical council met on December 14.

"If our credits are not accepted, we'll be eating grass like the kangaroo."

"Or eucalyptus leaves like the koala bear." Etta laughed. "But look how God has led so far. If we had stayed in Honolulu another month——"

They were to see still more of God's leading.

On December 14 the state council committee met. Many medical heads looked askance at the Kresses' credentials. Some of the men were plainly against their acceptance, and there was a reason.

One member announced, "We shall not accept these Americans. It's not in accordance with the new law."

"But their credits are good. They have reciprocity with our requirements."

"You mean they did have until December 7. New South Wales has passed a law refusing all diplomas other than those of English sanction. I'm sorry."

"But, sir, the council at Sydney already accepted these credentials before this law was passed."

"Is that verified?"

"Definitely. The date was November 14, sir."

Then without hesitation the director said, "In this case I move that the doctors from America be accepted. We are fortunate to have their help. But because this law is now in effect, this will be the last acceptance by this board of doctors without English degrees or reciprocity. Is that clear?"

It was clear, in more ways than one. It was clear to all that God had led them. The Kresses knelt to thank a wise heavenly Father, who knows all about the laws, present or future.

"Out of the Depths"

*A*RE YOU sure it was Avondale school, Mable?"

Ora Kress, now just thirteen years old, strained to hear the answer. Her keen ear had caught the name Avondale in the conversation between two elderly ladies sitting behind her on the train from Sydney.

"Of course, I'm sure it was Avondale. She said the students there are nearly starved. Why, they get only two meals a day. No meat, mind you, and no tea or coffee."

The first voice ground to a halt, but the second voice picked up the tempo.

"Don't they realize that growing children need meat to be healthy?"

Ora's ears tingled. She moved restlessly in her seat.

"And they say most of the students work their way. They need good food. It's a shame."

Finally Ora turned around. Her pretty face flushed pink, contrasting nicely with her dark hair and eyes. "Pardon me for listening to your conversation, ladies," she interrupted, "but I couldn't help hearing what you said. The word *Avondale* caught my ear. I go to school there."

"You do? Oh, you poor thing!" The lady was tall and thin with a little squeaky voice. She leaned forward, wanting to hear more.

"You don't need to feel sorry for me. It's a wonderful

school, really. Someone has misinformed you. We are all well
and happy there. Look at me! Do I look sickly? I've never
tasted meat in my life."

"Well, I declare! You do look healthy and pretty as a picture—and you don't drink tea or coffee either?" It was the fat
lady speaking this time. "Tell me," she began——

Ora spoke up quickly. "Yes, ma'am, I'll be glad to tell you.
My father and mother are both doctors. They'll be practicing
at the Sydney Sanitarium when it's finished. I've heard them
lecture lots of times."

"Do tell!" the thin lady exclaimed.

"They've lectured in America and England and now here.
We're all vegetarians, too. It may seem like something new,
but it isn't really. It was the perfect diet that God gave to
Adam and Eve in the Garden of Eden. Then when the Flood
covered the earth with water and everything was killed, God
permitted men to kill animals for food."

"Well, that is what the Bible says." The tall one nodded
her head.

Ora went on. "The animals at that time were healthy. Even
then there were only certain animals that God allowed them to
eat. We just don't need meat today, even if it were healthful.
We've found that tea and coffee are harmful, so that's why we
don't use them. You ought to come and visit our place. You
could have a good meal at the cafeteria and stay for a lecture."

"Well, bless you, we will. It looks as if Mable and I could
both use some health lectures. She's too fat, and I'm all skin
and bones. It was a pleasure to meet you, young lady."

"My name is Kress—Ora Kress."

"You mean you are the Kresses' daughter? What a coinci-
dence!"

Nowhere had the Kress family been more royally welcomed
than on this beautiful continent. Here the people, both rich and

poor, seemed eager to learn the new health discoveries that were sweeping into other countries. Here most of the people were hard-working, heavy-meat-eating people with a habitual tradition of tea and coffee drinking. Here where fruit was so abundant the supply of fresh meat was also plentiful.

One day Daniel received a letter from the president of the conference at Sydney. It stated, "Your work and that of your wife have been most encouraging. We are hearing of the good results of your lectures and of your wife's cooking classes.

"Until the sanitarium in Sydney is ready to open, would you folk consider coming to our aid in Cooranbong? We have a Health Retreat there that needs new management. It's seventy-five miles from Sydney.

"It is not a large place—only fifteen beds—but there will be plenty for both of you to do, with outside calls in neighboring areas. It may be more rural than you are used to, but I think you will like it. This is a real challenge, both financially and medically."

A letter came back promptly in Etta's neat handwriting: "We accept the challenge of the Health Retreat at Cooranbong, but we want it understood that if it does not pay off financially, we will accept no salary."

Then Lauretta, the manager, took over. Her smile as she opened her first letter from the conference was an indication of the contents. Happy and proud of her accomplishment for the previous month, Etta gaily waved the check in the air.

"Look, Dan! We did it!"

"What would I do without my little manager? Etta—Lauretta——" Dan's voice suddenly sounded shaky and unsure, like a teen-age boy whose voice was changing. "Etta, I don't know how to tell you this. I—I hate to tell you. It—it isn't fair."

Etta looked confused. "What are you saying, Dan? What isn't fair?"

Dan didn't answer. Instead he put his head in his hands and sobbed like a child.

"Dan, Dan, whatever is wrong, dear?" Standing over her husband like a fond mother, she leaned his head against her and let him weep. She stroked his hair, his throbbing temples, his heavy eyebrows.

Raising his head, Dan forced himself to speak. "And it's you, you who must take all the responsibilities, you who must carry all the burdens that I should carry——"

Was Dan jealous of her capabilities? Was he hurt because she had managed the Health Retreat? The questions flashed like little pricks of lightning through the mind of Lauretta Kress.

But Dan never had a jealous hair in his head. That couldn't be the reason!

"Etta, I'm sorry. I didn't want to tell you. I didn't want to hurt you."

"Dan, look at me, dear. You haven't told me a thing. But I suspect. Look at me, Dan!"

Dan obeyed.

"Daniel Kress, you're sick again. Oh, sweetheart, I'm so sorry." Etta hid her face in his arms. "Forgive me for not seeing. I've been so busy trying to prove myself a good manager again."

"I know, Etta. I've never been so discouraged before." The sobs started again. Then lifting his head, Dan went on. "Where have I failed? I've tried so hard to be a true witness to these people, but this is a reproach to what we believe."

"Dan, Dan! I've never heard you talk like this before. I won't let you be discouraged. It's a destructive thing. No one knows the cause of anemia. You're just punishing yourself. We need to think again how God has led us here. He directed about our credentials. The new sanitarium is about to open. I know He wants us there. Now——"

"Yes, yes, I know, Etta; but I can't stand to have you carry all the burden again."

"Dan, I'm a healthy, happy woman. I love my work. I love you. Come on now, cheer up. I'll fix you a good supper, and tomorrow we will see the doctor. Look! The sun is shining."

The supper was a disappointment. Even the fresh fragrance of the roses on the table received feeble mention.

Weeks dragged into months for this pioneer whose hope seemed to be a silken gossamer thread stretched tautly into space. Face to face with the Grim Reaper, Daniel's faith was sorely tried. He grew steadily weaker.

Lauretta, constantly fresh and buoyant, tried every device to tempt Dan's appetite. One morning she had slipped into his room just after breakfast-time. His tray, still untouched, caught her eye.

"Good morning, dear," she said softly. "What a nice breakfast. Your favorite—applesauce. Come on, try a spoonful. O.K.?"

"Etta, don't force me. I have no appetite. What is going to happen to us?" Dan took her hand in his, stroking it gently. "How can I go on like this?" His voice was quivering and weak.

Brave Etta brightened. She even forced a light laugh. "Come on, Dan. Do you want me to send your food to the starving Chinese? Here's a spoonful for Ora—she sends her love. She'll drop by after a while. . . . Say, you ought to see the geranium hedge. Remember how you trimmed it? Well, it's a beauty. . . . Here's a sip of apricot juice. Good! Drink it all now. . . . I must tell you what happened yesterday. It was so comical. . . . This toast looks good, dear. I'll cut a piece for you. . . . Well, as I was saying, this tall man came into the office with his wife. 'I want the doctor,' he said. So I answered, 'I'm the doctor.'

" 'I don't know if you'll do or not.' He looked me up and down. . . . Here, try the rest of this juice, dear. . . .

"So I said, 'Tell me what you want, and I'll see if I can help you.'

" 'I have a bad tooth, and I want it pulled out,' he told me.

"You know, Dan, I've never pulled a tooth in all my life, but I did it! It wasn't so bad either.

"When he asked, 'Is it out?' I showed it to him.

" 'You're a brick,' he said. 'Do you know you're the third person who's tried to pull that tooth out?' . . . Here is the rest of that toast. . . .

"Did I tell you about my new profession?"

"New profession?" Dan asked.

"Yes. Yesterday morning a man asked me to help him with his sick horse. Colic."

Dan smiled, unbelieving.

"Yes, colic! I told him I was not much of a horse doctor, but I gave him some Epsom salts and sent Jim along with some gunnysacks and an old blanket. They sewed the sacks together, dipped the blanket in hot water and wrung it out, and fastened them all around the horse. . . . Oh, look! You've cleaned up your tray, Dan! . . . Oh, yes, back to the horse." Etta seemed pleased about her accomplishment. "Jim said they left this morning, so I guess the horse was all right."

"Etta, whom do you think you're fooling? So I ate a dab of food. What happens now? I'm getting weaker every day. You can see that, and so can I. Maybe the Lord wants me to die. If so, I'm ready. I'm so tired."

Dr. Lauretta looked surprised, but she didn't comment. "I'll be up every chance I get, dear." Then she smiled brightly. "Oh, I nearly forgot your mail. One of the letters is from Michigan. Tell me about it when I come up again. I must hurry, Dan."

Brave, busy little doctor. Triumphantly she carried the empty tray to the kitchen. Dan's words followed her: "Etta, whom are you fooling?" She had helped him eat a tiny dish of applesauce, a bite of toast, a few sips of apricot juice. So what had been accomplished? Her triumph was short-lived. Suddenly she wanted to be alone, to weep without anyone seeing. To see her husband steadily losing the battle was disheartening enough, but to think of his utter lack of a desire to live was a different thing. Would she and Ora be deprived of their most precious possession?

"What can I do, God? It's awful to see him so discouraged, to see him so thin, so weak," Etta pleaded. "How can we go on like this? Show us Your way. Help us to know what to do. This is Your work. Give us Your wisdom, dear God."

"Dr. Kress!" someone called into the kitchen. "Has anyone seen Dr. Lauretta?"

Quickly the little doctor dried her tears.

"Are you calling me?"

"Oh, yes, ma'am. Dr. Daniel wants you right away, please."

Etta hurried up the steps to her husband's room. Out of breath, she panted, "Dan, what is it, dear?"

Dan's voice was feeble. "Elder Robinson—wants—to—see—you." As he spoke, a thin-faced man arose from the chair by the window. Etta looked surprised as she shook his hand.

"I do want to talk with you, Doctor; but could we have prayer here with Daniel first?"

Heads were bowed, hearts were blended, and voices were lifted in earnest petition. Then bidding Daniel good-bye, Elder Robinson walked down the hall with Etta. He spoke anxiously. "I couldn't believe my eyes, Doctor. You have a very sick husband."

"I know."

"He seems to believe he is dying."

"What can we do, Elder Robinson? I can't believe God brought us here for this."

"Daniel hasn't been anointed, has he?"

"No."

"We need him desperately. I can't feel that it's God's will for him to die. I can call the brethren. What time——"

"Dr. Lauretta!" A nurse interrupted, hurrying toward them. "Dr. Kress wants to see you both. He says it's important!"

They hurried back to his room. Daniel whispered feebly, "Etta, I noticed this letter again. The—one—from—Michigan. It's Mrs. White's handwriting. Open it—and—read—it—please."

Anxiously Lauretta began to read:

"May 29, 1901

"Dear Brother and Sister Kress:

"I am deeply pained to learn that Brother Kress is ill. We have not yet heard the particulars. I have some things I wish to send you if I can get them off in this mail. Several cases have been presented to me, which I shall speak of in due time; meanwhile, do not put yourself through as you have done and do not go to extremes in regard to the health reform.

"When you see that you are becoming weak physically, it is essential for you to make changes, and at once. Put into your diet something you have left out. It is your duty to do this. Get eggs of healthy fowls. Use these eggs cooked or raw. Drop them uncooked into the best unfermented wine you can find. This will supply that which is necessary to your system. Do not for a moment suppose that it will not be right to do this. . . .

"The prayer of faith shall save the sick, and I beseech you to call for the elders of the church without delay. May the Lord help you, is my most sincere prayer. We appreciate your experience as a physician, and yet I say that milk and eggs should be included in your diet. These things cannot at present be dispensed with, and the doctrine of dispensing with them should not be taught. . . .

"Brother and Sister Kress, I have all confidence in you, and I greatly desire that you may have physical health, in order that you may have perfect soundness spiritually. It is lack of suitable food that has caused you to suffer so keenly. You have not taken the food essential to nourish your frail physical strength. You must not deny yourself of good, wholesome food. . . .

"You love to obey the commandments of God. . . . God calls for whole-souled, upright, high-principled men. These are the men needed in our institutions. Those who are satisfied with half-and-half service can well be spared.

"I arose very early this morning and wrote the foregoing before breakfast. I have more written on the subject which the next mail may bring to you."*

It was a solemn time. Realizing that this letter had already been on the ocean several weeks, Lauretta whispered reverently, "Before we called, He answered; and while we were yet speaking, He heard."

After a prayer of thanks for God's guidance, Etta seemed to gain courage. "This is the first bit of hope we've had. Elder Robinson, will you arrange for the anointing?"

"Gladly. I'll also wire the General Conference and our brethren in England. Can we set a day of prayer next Sabbath and have the anointing in the afternoon at two o'clock?"

Then Dan spoke. "I'm sorry I've made so much trouble for everyone. Notify the folks in New Zealand and Tasmania, especially Brother Murphet. I'm ashamed of my little faith, Etta. I feel so unworthy."

Lauretta stooped to kiss her husband tenderly. Carefully she put the letter between the pages of the Bible which always lay handy on Dan's bedside table.

There was a new vigor in her step, a new courage in her eyes, a new determination to make these days bright and fruitful.

11

From the office of the conference president went out a cablegram: "Kress dying. Pray. All churches, Sabbath, June 15, 1901."

On the appointed day the ministers and their wives came to petition the Great Physician for the health of this man who was so much needed.

"Etta, take my hand," he whispered. "My faith is so small. I want this letter from Mrs. White to be read again before we pray. I do want to do all I know to be right. Sorry I was doing wrong. God help me."

The letter of advice was read. The prayers of faith were offered. The oil of anointing was spread on the pale forehead. Many tears were shed around the circle of the globe that Sabbath afternoon. Daniel and Lauretta Kress, like all the others, awaited the answer.

In the darkness that night, Dan was wide-eyed and wondering. His sleepless gaze took in the velvet beauty of the sky set with stars. Where were the Big Dipper and Orion?

Then remembering he was in a different hemisphere, he started to study the skies earnestly. Each night by his window Dan renewed his acquaintance with the stars. Each night the miracle of God's wisdom impressed itself upon his mind. Each night he talked to his Maker, thanking Him over and over for the desire to live, asking for faith to step into the future.

Two weeks crept slowly into eternity. The third Sabbath Dan got up, dressed, and walked to church service. When an opportunity came, Dan stood to his feet, and with all eyes upon him he told his story.

"I feel as Lazarus must have felt," he began, "or the son of the widow of Nain. I never thought I would again be in this church to speak to you. I want to thank you all for your prayers for me. Your faith has made up for my lack. I dedicate the years of my life that are left to Him who healed me. I want to read you one verse, Acts 4:14: 'And beholding the man which was healed standing with them, they could say nothing against it.' "

Dan's new faith grew as his health prospered. His color was good, and the laboratory reports looked encouraging. Many people were watching Daniel Kress. Some declared he would get better for a while, then lose ground again. They were to be disappointed.

One day early in July, Dan reached into the mailbox for their daily mail. As he walked into the house, he called, "Lauretta, there's a letter for you from England."

"England?" Etta seemed surprised. She started to read aloud:

" 'My dear Mrs. Kress: I have just heard of the death of our dear Dr. Kress——' " Etta stopped, shocked. "O Dan! We never wrote to them again, after the day of the special prayer! Oh, how awful! Dan, they think—this is a letter of condolence!" Etta threw her arms around Dan and started to cry. "I can never be thankful enough that you're better. But we must call Elder Robinson immediately. We must notify these dear people. How human can we be! I'm so sorry, dear."

As the cables had gone out for help, so the cables went out again in gratitude for the prayers which had been united all over the world to bring healing.

A tiny pebble of thanks was thrown into the ocean. Wider and wider it circled, until it reached the shores of New Zealand and Tasmania. Its currents, like the Gulf Stream, embroidered a lacy scallop of foam along many shores. America, England, Pitcairn, Honolulu, even Scotland and Ireland, heard its song of praise.

"God has heard our prayers. In union there is strength. We have prayed as one family, and we have been answered as one family. Thank God!"

Dr. Daniel Kress's work was not done. He was yet to bring emancipation to people who were still shackled by the habits of a lifetime. Could he see today the magazines, the newspapers, the radio and television broadcasts, that tell the world, "Tobacco is your enemy! Smoke at your own risk!" how happy he would be to think of the work the Lord spared him to do.

Ellen G. White Letter 37, 1901. A portion of this letter was published in *Counsels on Diets and Foods,* p. 203, and in *Medical Ministry,* pp. 286, 287.

Walk On, Walk On

*T*HE OPEN HOUSE of Wahroonga Sanitarium on December 1, 1902, was a grand, joyful occasion. Some of those who attended were ill, some well, some famous, some ignoble, a few fashionable, and many ordinary; but each was happy because of the occasion which brought them together. Surely the health of the entire community would benefit from this garden spot of Sydney. The buildings were spacious, with comfortable verandas encircling each. The hospital proper was constructed in the center of a large orchard. When it was in full bloom, the place was a restful delight.

The student nurses, brisk and fresh in their new uniforms, served as the hostesses for the occasion. The program was solemn and inspiring. God must have been pleased with the happy atmosphere.

One thing was giving special concern to the Kresses, who were responsible for the hospital's management. The building fund was completely depleted. Yet the much-needed treatment rooms had no equipment at all.

Daniel was much disturbed. During a visit with the conference president one day he suggested a way out. "I'd like to visit Mr. Murphet in Tasmania. He is a friend of mine, and he's always been very generous."

The president stood to his feet. "Whatever you do, I beg you, Doctor, don't ask that man for money. He's old, and he has helped us so much already. I think he's becoming suspicious that we're only interested in his money. You understand?"

Dan replied, "I won't ask him for a cent. But I can pray that the Lord will impress him of our needs; and if he should want to help, I couldn't refuse him!"

Dan's visit with his old friend was most pleasant. After an hour of friendly conversation, Dan stood up to leave. "My train leaves soon," Dan said. "Brother, I guess it's good-bye for this time. Someday before long there will be no more good-byes."

Cane in hand, the old gentleman walked Dan to the door. He smiled almost quizzically. "Doctor, haven't you forgotten something?"

"Forgotten? What do you mean, Mr. Murphet?"

Mr. Murphet chuckled. His long and happy life had put wrinkles of pleasure in the right place on his round, pink face. "Well, don't you need some money?"

Dan laughed. "Yes, the Lord's work always needs money."

"Come now, how much do you need?"

Dan took a deep breath. Did he dare? "Well, we need $10,000 to equip the treatment room and finish the sanitarium," he finally blurted.

"I have notes in that amount coming due in a few days. I'll be glad to let you have it, without interest. When the hospital is prosperous, then you can pay 3 percent; and when I die, you may keep it all!"

"You're an answer to our prayers," Dan said gratefully. Not only did this generous man give $10,000 then, but later he gave an additional $5,000. God was still looking after His hospital.

The sun shone warmly on the campus. The orchard was like a Garden of Eden, producing luscious peaches, plums, pomegranates, persimmons, oranges, lemons, mulberries, and nectarines. Feeling like Adam and Eve, Dan and Etta walked in their garden, taking great pride in the work of their own hands. Every morning from five until eight o'clock they spent in their garden. The work was good for them, and the results were obvious.

"I love this place," Dan remarked. "I'd just as soon live here the rest of my life." He leaned contentedly on the handle of his hoe.

A twinkle gleamed in Etta's eye. "Would you like your son to be an English citizen?" she asked nonchalantly.

Dan's mouth opened wide in surprise. "My son? An Englishman! You mean—you are——"

"Yes, I mean—— Well, it may not be a son, but——"

"I'd be the happiest man on earth!"

"We've always wanted a son, so I hope it *will* be a boy," Etta declared. "Won't this be some experience now, after all these years?"

Dan grinned mischievously at his wife. "And whom did you say you'd have for your obstetrician, madam?"

In May, 1902, little John was born. He was a perfect baby, the answer to any parent's prayer. Dan's joys knew no bounds. The whole world looked like a different place. It had a new purpose, an aim, a reality, a direction.

Every evening as he hurried home from the office, Dan's one thought was to scoop his little son into his arms. To forget the world of human woes and to lose himself in a child's world of wonder and curiosity was his delight. To marvel anew at each amazing development, to dream daily of the possibilities in this tiny intellect, was no small thrill.

"Little man, you've had a busy day," Dan would sing as the little fellow dropped his toys to creep wildly to the door, a welcoming committee of one.

"John, my Jo-John," Dan would chant each morning as he slid his son into the high chair, sweet, fresh, and hungry as usual. Dan tied the bib about John's neck and gave him a cracker to stop the banging of the spoon on the tray. Before long, happy blue eyes sparkled as the boy waved a pink-fisted good-bye to his father.

"Throw daddy a kiss, Jo-John."

But "da-da" was the only response; so Dan went happily on his way to the hospital.

One morning just before noon Dan had a caller. It was Etta, white-lipped and crying hysterically.

"Dan—it's John!"

Dan froze with fear. "Etta, what's happened?"

"He—he's in the hospital. He fell out of the high chair. O Dan—he fell—on his—head." Etta sobbed.

Grabbing Etta's hand, together they ran to the little boy's room.

John was unconscious and still as death. His head was bleeding badly, and the left side of his tiny body was paralyzed. Now what would they do?

Anxious hours were spent in constant prayers, some audible, some silent. Hours of sleepless watching stretched into days of anxiety. There were long vigils and hurried visits. The squeaking rocker by the bedside was an eerie monologue that seemed to go on and on.

Then one day John sat up, all alone with a little coaxing. Flagging spirits revived. All the anxious days of waiting seemed suddenly worthwhile. A whole year had passed since the accident. Like a patchwork quilt, those days and nights were a combination of love, patience, and despair.

One day that patience paid off. John walked. His left arm still hung limp and useless at his side, but the helpful hand of his father was within reach of John's good hand. Each step was an exciting experience for the father, as well as for the little son. Dan hugged John happily and wept a few tears of joy. The tiny fingers reached up to touch daddy's cheek. Perhaps John wondered why his daddy felt like crying.

"My son, my son, my little Jo-John." Pressing the soft cheek against his own, Dan wept afresh.

Would this son yet fulfill his father's dreams? Dan and Etta walked on together, accepting this trial that seemed more bitter than any other they had experienced.

As Enoch walked with God, as little John walked with his small hand in the comforting hand of his father, so the Kresses tried to walk with their faith secure in the Hand above.

The land "down under" became home to these transplanted Americans.

Now another challenge came to them through the mail. Would they be interested in returning to the United States and taking charge of the new Washington Sanitarium, near the nation's capital? The idea was appealing, and the need was urgent.

Another letter crossed the great ocean. The answer it carried was affirmative.

Unforgettable Lauretta

*J*T'S THAT circumcision you did earlier this morning, Dr. Lauretta," the nurse explained. "The little fellow must be a hemophiliac. I thought you'd want to check him before you leave."

"I'm glad you caught me, Miss Littlefield. I can check him right now."

The spry little doctor walked briskly toward the surgical wing. What stories she could tell of the happenings at Washington Sanitarium since she and Dan had come here twenty-two years before from Australia!

She remembered clearly the night of the hospital's grand opening, for she had helped to arrange the furniture in every room. Upon inspection, just as the guests were beginning to arrive, she was horrified to find that the third floor had been neglected.

"Oh, no!" she cried. "The beds—no one has made up the beds on this floor!"

Quickly she corralled a stray nurse in the hall, and they ran to the linen closet. Snatching the linen they needed, they scrambled through the bed-making process. Four speedy hands did the job quickly and neatly. When the guests began their inspection tour, everything was in order. Few listeners relaxed so completely during the dedication as did Lauretta and her helper.

The Washington Sanitarium and Hospital was an imposing building, even in 1929. Wide verandas provided an open view of the wooded hillside, which sloped down to the musical creek known as the Sligo. Paths led to the rocky ravine. Occasional benches invited tired guests to rest in the shade along the wooded trail.

This choice location was eight miles from the nation's Capitol. The big problem in the beginning was providing transportation for the patients. In winter the country roads were almost impassable. Patients were met at the end of the streetcar line by a surrey and a team of horses; or if they chose to come by rail, at the Baltimore and Ohio railway station.

Those were struggling days. In later years the campus was enlarged to include Washington Missionary College and its circle of buildings, pleasant walks, and a large tennis court. Each year brought more innovations. A large new hospital building eventually replaced the old chapel-gymnasium. In later years a collegiate nurse's training program replaced the original three-year course. These things were important, but for the present Dr. Lauretta was concerned about her small patient.

Swinging open the nursery door, the nurse hurried to the baskets of squealing babies. She read a name aloud, "Davies—Boy." "This is the one," she said, and laid him on the examining table.

"Well now, Mr. Davies." Dr. Lauretta's brown eyes twinkled. She was a brisk, happy person, always at ease in her work. Removing the diaper and the dressings, she said anxiously, "I guess you really are a bleeder. My, my! A few stitches here will take care of the problem. You can bring the emergency cart, Miss Littlefield, and we'll fix him in a hurry. Your name *is* Littlefield, isn't it?"

"That's right, Doctor. The first baby I ever saw delivered was one of yours."

"Really? That would be almost three years ago." Lauretta's keen eyes glowed with remembrance behind the round metal-rimmed glasses. Efficiently she began suturing her tiny patient.

"I guess that was about baby number 3,450." Miss Littlefield smiled as she handed Lauretta the sutures.

"That was in the days before the new delivery room," Lauretta recalled.

"Yes, and I think they were having another delivery at the time, because the regular nurses were busy, and I was asked to help hold the patient during the last part of her labor. I think I felt every pain that woman had."

"It's always a thrill to see a baby born. I never get tired of it."

"You know what I did?"

"I could guess."

"I went down to the dormitory room and collapsed on the bed. I cried as I had never cried before."

"I can understand that. It's wonderful work, though, isn't it? Now that should take care of this boy." She handed him back to Miss Littlefield. "If there's any more trouble, call me. By the way, I have a case due today—a girl thirteen, un-wed——"

"Thirteen?"

"It's such a sad case. The parents don't even want the girl to see the baby. I thought you should know so you can tell the others."

Back at the nurses' desk, Miss Littlefield handed a stack of charts to the doctor, who left her orders quickly. "Miss Littlefield, please call the registry for the special nurse for 110. If you need me, I'll be in surgery. Mrs. McKensie is having her twins today, you know, by caesarean. There's a sick woman. She had a convulsion this morning. You'll probably need another special for her. Better notify the registry as soon as you can."

"Yes, I know. Dr. Truman already told us. Thank you."

Quickly the nurse turned to place the call to the registry, but was too late. The phone was already ringing.

"Maternity, Miss Littlefield. . . . Yes, we're expecting you. . . . Yes, Dr. Kress is in the building now. . . . All right, we'll tell her you're on the way. Good-bye."

Quickly she dialed delivery room. "Mildred? . . . Good news! . . . She's on her way up now. Just called. Dr. Lauretta's in surgery. By the way, she asked me to tell you girls—this patient is thirteen years old. The parents asked that she not see the baby. I thought you ought to know. . . . Thanks, Mildred."

It was time for rounds with the doctors. Medications and examinations—hospitals are busy places.

"Miss Littlefield!"

"Yes, Miss Price."

"Have you seen Dr. Lauretta yet this morning?" Miss Price, the ward nurse, motioned to Miss Littlefield to close the door.

"When you see the doctor, will you send her in to see Mrs. Denton? She insists that she will not nurse her baby. I told her she should be glad she can. But she's afraid she will lose her figure! It makes me so mad!" Her black eyes snapped as she spoke.

"If Dr. Kress wants that baby on a formula, we will need to order one. But if I know Dr. Lauretta, that baby will probably be nursing from its mother by tonight!" Miss Price breezed down the hall and out of sight. Miss Littlefield made a note on her memo pad and hurried back to the nurses' station.

About five minutes later the swinging doors to the maternity suite opened with their usual squeak. Three worried and frightened-looking people stood on the threshold. One was a very young blonde girl. She was carrying a burden that no thirteen-year-old should have to carry. She sighed wearily as a tall, thin man beside her stepped up to speak to the nurse in charge.

"This is Patricia, Dr. Lauretta's patient. I called a few minutes ago. This is her mother, and I'm her father."

"I'm glad to see you. Suppose we get Patricia settled in her room, and then I'll call Dr. Lauretta. You folks can wait in the waiting room. We'll call you when we get things arranged."

After calling surgery to alert the doctor, the nurse took the girl to the labor room. The parents' eyes haunted her. As she turned back the linen on the bed, she was glad they were alone. What could she say to a girl like Patricia?

"Here's your gown, Patricia. Hop into bed. The doctor will be here in a minute."

"I'm scared to death." Her voice shook.

"Don't be afraid. You have the best doctor in the country."

"I know, but I can't even have my own baby———"

"Maybe it'll be better that way, Patricia. Look ahead a few years. You can go back and finish school. Show the world you're a wonderful woman. One mistake doesn't need to spoil a lifetime."

Patricia nodded. "Another pain! Let me hold your hand, nurse!"

The door opened, and Dr. Lauretta's happy smile seemed to light up the room.

"Here's the lady you want to see," the nurse told Patricia. To the doctor she said, "I'll see you in delivery."

"You did call the registry for the special?"

"Yes. Did Mrs. McKensie have the twins?"

"Twin boys. They look identical. Now—let's see about this young lady."

Passing the delivery room on her way to lunch, Miss Little-field thought about Patricia. In the scrub room she found Mildred, the delivery room nurse.

"How's Patricia doing?"

"Last stage—should deliver any time now."

Peeping through the open door, she saw the usual. Dr. Lauretta was in command, confident and happy, letting nature take its course. "You're doing fine, Patricia," she was saying. "I can see your baby's head right now. We'll give you a little something to help you with these next pains. Just a few more, and it will all be over." Then Dr. Lauretta continued her casual conversation with the nurses.

"Dr. Dan just will not drive the car. I've had him behind the wheel, but every time a car passes him, he throws up his hands and I have to grab the steering wheel. . . . Now, Patricia, make this one count. Press down! That's good! Just a few more like that, and we can all have some dinner. . . . So I said to him when he did it again, 'Now just what would you do if you were the only one in the car at the top of a hill? Suppose the car should start to roll down the hill. What would you do, Daniel?'

"He answered, 'I'd blow the horn!' "

Everyone laughed. The doctor nodded to the anesthetist. "Give her more gas. She should have some help now."

The anesthetist responded. The next pain was sharp and rewarding, and suddenly the baby was born. Dr. Lauretta was sure that baby's cry was the most welcome sound this side of heaven.

"A perfect boy!" she announced. But Patricia couldn't hear the doctor's words. "A beautiful baby, and she's not even to see it. What a pity!"

At 2:30 in the afternoon office hours began for Dr. Lauretta. The waiting room was crowded as usual. Women of all ages were happy to have a capable doctor who could understand their needs.

A large screen, used as a room divider, was the center of

interest in this office. It was the conversation piece, for on this screen were pictures of all the babies Dr. Lauretta had delivered.

"Look at the twins!" someone commented.

"This is a cute baby."

"Look, Jan; there's Betty's baby. I think I will send the doctor one of us when our little fellow comes."

The friend laughed. "Little fellow? It may be girl triplets!"

"If I had a dozen, I'd still want Dr. Lauretta! Wouldn't you?"

Dr. Lauretta was obviously loved, admired, and trusted by all her patients. But nowhere was she loved and admired more than in her own home. John, although he was twenty-eight years old, still lived with his parents. The tragic fall from the high chair when he was just a baby had severely damaged his brain. Although he had developed physically, his mind had remained in childhood. He could talk well, however, and enjoyed many of the same activities of an average child. He was particularly fascinated by crayons and color books.

"Mother, what color is my Taffy dog?"

"This color, John." Lauretta handed him the brown crayon.

"Then is this Blackie's color?"

"That's right."

"And this one is the same as your dress." He picked up a pretty blue one. "It's nice to have you home, Mother. Come sit by me. I love you."

Lauretta smiled at her son. "I love you too, Jo-John."

The living room door opened, and Dan came in, smiling, but looking a little tired after his busy day at the hospital.

"Hello, dear. Have a good day?" Etta asked as he made himself comfortable in his favorite chair.

"About the usual. How about you?"

"O Dan, the funniest thing happened today. We had a caesarean section this morning. I was taking one of the babies

12

down to the nursery, and I saw a tiny little old lady in the waiting room. Thinking it might be the grandmother, I said to her, 'Wouldn't you like to see our little caesarean baby?'

"She stood on tiptoe to peek at him and then got the most puzzled look on her face.

" 'It's a sweet baby, all right,' she said, 'but tell me something.'

" 'Of course,' I said. 'What would you like to know?'

"Seriously she replied, 'What nationality is caesarean?' "

Dan and Etta enjoyed a good laugh together. It was nice to relax in the privacy of the family circle.

"Any mail?" Dan inquired.

"Oh, I almost forgot. We got a letter from Ora, and she sent some pictures." Lauretta hurried to bring him the envelope.

There were pride and happiness in Dan's face as he looked at the pictures. Ora had become the fulfillment of parental dreams for both Dan and Etta. She had worked hard to finish her medical training and had married a fellow physician, William Mason, shortly after her graduation. Their little girl, Patricia, was the pride and joy of two very fond grandparents.

Dan's face glowed with happiness as he read his daughter's letter. God was good. He had worked out the puzzle of life in a very rewarding way. Proudly Dan set the new photograph up on the mantel. He straightened his tired shoulders. With children like his, a man had reason to walk tall.

A Day With Dr. Dan

*I*T WAS 8:00 A.M.: "So you hid my hat, did you?"

Dr. Dan rumpled the stubby hair on his son's head as he spoke. A smile played about his lips.

John nodded, grinning. "I don't want you to leave, Daddy."

"I know, John; but who else can take care of Senator Capper? Come now, you don't want your father to catch cold without a hat."

"Oh, no, Daddy. Here it is. I was only fooling." Reluctantly John handed over the missing hat.

"Thanks, John." Dan always kissed his son before he left in the morning.

"I'll pray for you today, Daddy. Tell Senator Capper hello for me, and Mrs. Leftner too, and don't forget about the night-blooming cereus. Mother said to invite everyone because tonight it's at its best. She called the newspaper, and they're coming out to take pictures."

"Well, it looks as if you'll have lots of excitement today, son. Don't forget to walk Taffy around the block."

Taffy, a cocker, sniffed at the doctor's heels. She knew she was being talked about. The boy and his dog watched as usual from the porch as Dr. Dan crossed the highway and turned to wave good-bye from the corner.

The uphill walk to the hospital was brisk. Dan breathed deeply of the sweet fresh air. His cheeks glowed as he entered the wide hallway by the patients' dining room. Here he encountered his favorite patient. Mrs. Leftner was inching along in her wheelchair.

"But, Mrs. Leftner, you should be at breakfast."

"Breakfast is for the birds! Don't you remember I'm trying to lose fifty pounds? Besides, my knees ached so much all night that I asked for a treatment this morning." She laughed heartily. Her round face was jolly, regardless of her pain. "You see, Doctor, I'm such a fat old lady that I don't want anyone to see me taking a treatment; so I go early and avoid the rush!"

Dan joined her chuckle. "I told you to cut down on that pecan pie. By the way, Mrs. Leftner, how does that analgesic balm work for you? Does it really help your knees?"

"So you smell my perfume, too? I reek with the stuff, but it helps a little."

"There's a new medication——"

"I'll try anything! Bring it up when you come, Doctor." The wheelchair squeaked its way to the elevator.

8:15: As he hurried down the hall, the doctor nearly collided with a peppy young callboy pushing an empty wheelchair.

"Walter!" Dan called, bending to rub his shin, "wait a minute."

"Oh, I'm sorry, Doctor. Did I hurt your leg? I didn't mean to cut that corner so sharp. Here, sit down in the wheelchair."

"No, no. I'm all right, I think. But, son, it's you I'm worried about."

"Me?"

"Maybe I could give you a word of advice. You should learn to avoid all bustle and flurry. Sick people want to move quietly. Anything else makes them restless and unsure. Make each move count. Jesus is a good example. Can you imagine Him rushing about?"

"No, sir. I never thought about that before. I'll remember, though, and I surely hope your leg will be all right."

The tall teen-ager smoothed his pace as he skillfully maneuvered his two-wheeled chariot down the hall and through the big doors to the runway.

Dr. Kress stepped into his office off the main hall that led to the patients' parlor. He found a pencil and a note pad and began jotting down a few notes. He bowed his head in his hands in a short prayer for guidance during the day ahead.

8:30: Music from the patients' parlor drifted pleasantly down the hall. It was time for the daily devotional service.

Dr. Dan rose to give the short inspirational thoughts. He always liked to illustrate his point with a story.

"A special train carrying commuting businessmen to a large city was sidetracked at a small station. After waiting a reasonable time, the men became restless, thinking of their impending appointments," he commented.

"One of them complained to the conductor, 'You're giving us terrible service. Don't you know we're all in a hurry?'

"The conductor made no reply, but he paced the aisle restlessly. A freight train going in the same direction passed them. This was more than the passengers could take. They demanded an explanation. The conductor was still silent. Time ticked away.

"Finally the door opened, and the conductor announced, 'Gentlemen, there has been a heavy rain in this area during the night. We all felt uncertain about the bridge. Word has come to us that the bridge has collapsed under the freight that you saw pass us a few minutes ago.'

"Life is like that. Often we find fault with Providence because we are temporarily sidetracked. Some of you may feel that way this morning. But don't be discouraged. Your stay here may be the one thing that will help you to have a long and happy life.

"Now, I have two important announcements to make. Tonight at 7:30 the famous Dr. J. H. Kellogg will speak here in this parlor. Don't miss it. The service will be on radio for those who cannot leave their beds. Then after that you're all invited to our home to see our night-blooming cereus with over one hundred blossoms on it. Our car will be available for any of you who would like to ride. Now, let us all stand and say the Mizpah together."

10:00: "My friend! Pastor Whitney, how good to see you!"

"I'm in trouble, Dr. Kress." The pastor sighed as he let his ponderous weight sag into the chair beside Dan's desk.

Dan leaned forward anxiously, studying the tired, unhappy face before him. "Tell me about it, Warren," he invited.

"There's not much to tell, Dr. Dan. The old battery needs a recharge, and the starter won't work anymore. You know, too much work and worry. We've just finished a new church—I guess it was more than I should have undertaken."

"How about your faith in God?"

"Never better. Nothing can change that, no matter what. I'm of good courage. Really, I think I just need to hear the music of the Sligo from a third-floor hospital room," the minister declared.

Dr. Dan could give a good physical examination. He also dispensed confidence and courage, and on the side even a gentle ribbing now and then.

"I'm going to be hard on you, Pastor," he said. "A lot of your trouble comes from lack of exercise, and overweight. What do you say we give you a brisk hydro treatment. Then I want you to walk each morning for one hour. Don't just stroll—walk fast. While you walk, breathe deeply. Inhale for ten steps, then exhale for ten. I want an afternoon walk for one hour, too. Eat fresh fruit for breakfast and supper. Let's get back to that 170 pounds I used to see on you. Oh, I nearly forgot about water— it's free, so use it between meals, eight glasses a day. Come down and talk to me each day. I enjoy visiting with you. And here's a new book you can read while you rest." That was the secret of Dr. Dan's success—good sense in everyday living.

11:00: A wheelchair nosed into the doctor's office. "Come in, Mrs. Anderson. You're looking better today."

"Oh, thank you, Doctor. I'm trying to do as you told me. I've quit reading so much. Guess it's too exciting for me. I do feel better. Guess what I am doing in my spare time."

"Have you joined the knitters?"

"No, I'm not a knitter. But look at the watercolors I've been doing!"

"Say, you've done a good job on these! They're beautiful. May I show them to the ladies in the physical therapy class? Come with me. You ought to meet these ladies. Maybe you can give them some ideas."

With that he pushed the wheelchair up to the elevator, and they disappeared.

In a few minutes he was back at his desk again. Dr. Dan was always writing. It was easier for him to string words together on paper than to say them aloud.

But the telephone interrupted, as usual. "Dr. Kress, this is the floor supervisor. I have a problem."

"Yes, Mrs. Henderson. I hope I can help."

"I'm sure you can. You know, you haven't seen Elder Spicer yet today."

"That's right, I haven't."

"I was in his room just now, and he seemed a little disheartened. That isn't like him. We all love him and try to watch him carefully, because he won't turn on his call light. He doesn't want to bother anyone. He needs to know someone needs him. Is there anything you can get him to do? He's having a lot of pain. Maybe you could order another treatment for him about bedtime. O.K.?"

"Thanks for reminding me. I can see him right now."

The doctor went right up to see Elder Spicer, who was suffering from an attack of arthritis. They spent a wonderful hour together, reminiscing, discussing a new book, praying together. When Dan left, it was hard to tell who had benefited the most from the visit. As the doctor was about to leave, Elder Spicer leaned forward to shake his hand. Something hard and metallic fell to the floor with a thud. Dr. Dan reached to pick it up. It was a small pair of pliers. What would Elder Spicer want with pliers?

"So you bring your tools along?" Dr. Kress laughed, handing the pliers to his friend. The elder grinned sheepishly.

"It's a trick of mine. With these I can pull on my own socks, and I don't have to bother anyone."

2:00 P.M.: Time for office hours. There was a quick knock on the doctor's door.

"Come!"

"I'm glad you're here, Dr. Kress." The young man sounded anxious. "May I see you a few minutes? It's very important." Jim Hanton fingered his hat nervously as he spoke.

"Sit down, Jim. I hear you chauffeured a trip to the Cumberlands over the weekend."

"That's what I want to talk to you about, sir. You know Mrs. Boynton? She has been your patient for months. Well, her husband just had surgery here."

"Yes, I know. Go on, Jim."

"Well, she wanted to go home. Of course he couldn't drive yet, so he asked me to drive her there and bring her back today. Now what can I tell him? She wasn't able to come back."

"You mean she was drunk again?"

"Yes. The housekeeper said there wasn't a drop in the house. Mr. Boynton had seen to that before he came here, but she called out for it Saturday night. She was clear under today. I couldn't even get her into the car. How am I going to tell him?

He's sitting out on the lawn now, waiting to surprise her. He thought she was cured. I can't tell him." Jim's brow furrowed.

"I'll go along, Jim. I'm glad you came to me. This will be a blow to him. He thought she was strong enough, but she wasn't. We have to lean hard on God sometimes, and I guess she hasn't come to that yet. These are some of the doctor's heartaches, but there are many triumphs, too. Don't let it discourage you. You are still planning to be a doctor, aren't you?"

Jim grinned as they walked out of the building to the lawn. "I was, but look at my hands now! I'm shaking like a leaf. Things like this take the wind out of my sails. I've been worried about it all day."

" 'God is a very present help.' Remember that, Jim. You were faithful in your responsibilities, and that's what really counts."

3:00: The telephone's incessant ringing greeted the doctor as he came back into his office.

"Yes, this is Dr. Kress."

"This is the floor supervisor again. I'm sure you know my voice by now, Doctor. We're having a bad time with your patient in 2118. She insists she's going home unless we give her another shot of morphine, and she's already called her folks to come and get her. Would you see what you can do, please?"

"Of course. It's a real struggle, but she must not go home now. In a day or so she'll be all right. I'll go right up. Thanks."

A light tap on the door of 2118 seemed to interrupt little of the telephone conversation. As the doctor stepped into the room, the girl was saying, ". . . and I can't stand this place another minute, Mother. If you don't come by suppertime, I'll take the bus——" The weeping voice continued, "Here's Dr. Kress now, and I'll tell him the same thing. Good-bye, Mother."

"Now, now. What's this I hear?" The smiling doctor took a seat in the chair near the bed. The light from the window highlighted his silver hair. The patient, a young married woman, was propped up in bed with many pillows. She was an attractive girl with dark hair and beautiful sad eyes. A cigarette still smoldered in the small dish on the table.

"That was my mother, Dr. Kress. I told her I'm going home." Her dark eyes hid behind long lashes as she fingered the bedspread nervously. "I can't stand it any longer without the medication."

"And yesterday you were so brave. Remember? I was proud of you. Now suppose you do go home tonight. The same friends will crowd around you, and you'll start right back on the dope again. What have you accomplished? You'll lose all that you have already gained. Am I right?"

The dark head nodded.

"But you told me you wanted to quit. You're the young lady who wants more than anything to be a good mother and a wife your husband can be proud of."

The dark eyes filled with tears. "Yes, Doctor, I do! I do! But how can I stand this—this—nervousness?"

"This is the hardest time; but if you'll work with us, we can help you. Your nurse can take you to the treatment room anytime. You see, it's your body crying out against the stuff you have been abusing it with. Mrs. Hunt, try to look ahead a few years. You'll either be an addict and destroy yourself, or a free woman that everyone will love. A mother with a sweet baby in her arms—that's what you want, isn't it?"

"Yes, Doctor. Oh, yes!"

"Then be willing to fight for it. Right now I want to have prayer with you. God can help you. He wants you to ask for His help. Pray all the harder when you are tempted to quit. After our prayer I want you and your nurse to take a brisk walk for half an hour. Then have a good sweating treatment and a vigorous hot and cold spray. Drink plenty of water and fruit juices. Your body needs to be washed clean inside of every trace of the dope. Gradually, then, the nerves will respond. Today may be the hardest day for you, but tell me now you'll stay and work it out. Your folks and your husband will be proud of you."

"I'll stay. I'll show them." The girl was determined now. "Pray for me, Dr. Kress. Then I'll call my mother."

"I've seen weaker ones than you win this same fight. You can win, too. Now let's pray."

The doctor smiled as he rose from his knees, and the patient smiled back at him. "The battle's as good as won," he said as he left. He heard the telephone receiver click from the hook. As the door slowly closed, the words he heard cheered him immensely.

"Mother, I'm sorry I'm such a baby. I've decided to stay. We'll overcome this thing yet. Pray for me. . . . I love you, too!"

"God, help her to be an overcomer," Dan prayed as he walked down the long hall to his office on the first floor.

6:00: At the staff supper that evening in the patients' dining room, Dr. J. H. Kellogg was the honored guest. The wide corridor was well lined with hospital employees and the many friends who wished to catch a glimpse of the famous physician. All eyes turned to see the little "czar" of the Battle Creek Sanitarium. Some of them had preconceived visions of a tall, dignified man with a flowing beard—perhaps a kingly sort, quiet and unassuming. They were to be disappointed.

7:30: Walking toward the parlor, the doctors presented quite a contrast. Tall, wavy-haired Dr. A. W. Truman, slim and humbly dignified, walked beside the "little Napoleon." Dr. Kellogg with his neatly cropped goatee hurried with small, quick steps to keep up with the long strides of his six-foot-three friend. Both men enjoyed the dramatic moment.

The rest of the staff, smiling and happy, followed in the

joyful procession into the parlor. The Kresses had the privilege of introducing their good friend to the guests. The little doctor was given the royal welcome he much deserved. Once the introductions were over, all ears were tuned to his cheerful, vibrant message. Courage, faith, and hope were united as the doctor spoke. Each hearer was inspired by his enthusiasm.

9:00: The evening was not quite over. The Kresses escorted their friends and patients to their home to see the rare night-blooming cereus.

The guests exclaimed delightedly at the imcomparable beauty of the glistening white flowers. Dan and Etta were proud of its beauty, and the joy of sharing it with their friends seemed to make it doubly beautiful.

The Kresses were genial hosts. Delicious refreshments and relaxing casual conversation highlighted the remainder of the evening.

When the last visitor had departed, Dan and Etta walked slowly up the stairs together. A door squeaked companionably. Bedroom lights flashed on, then off again. Another day had ended for two busy, devoted doctors. The love and faithfulness of many people had helped to make it a good day for both of them.

Pause to Praise

𝒯HE TRAFFIC LIGHT on the corner in Takoma Park, Maryland, blinked its big red eye. The family car driven by Mrs. Haviland gave a sudden lurch.

"Meritta! Melinda! Maelene!" the mother gasped, thrusting her free right hand in front of her small daughters. The car stopped obediently, complaining a little like a naughty child.

A good-looking lady with *her* three small children in tow started to cross the street in front of the Haviland car.

Mrs. Haviland rolled down the window and called, "Pardon me, but could you direct me to the Kress residence?"

"Oh, certainly. Are you going to their anniversary party? We are. Say, why don't we come along and show you the way?" With a smile she and the children climbed into the back seat.

Meritta, Melinda, and Maelene are not fictional names. They were very functional babies—genuine triplets. They were introduced to the world by Dr. Lauretta, and this was undoubtedly the biggest party they had ever attended. Their big brown eyes danced with the Japanese lanterns that surrounded the whole yard and swayed in the breeze on that hot July 9, 1934.

"Here are my girls!" Dr. Lauretta beamed happily as she greeted her guests at the fiftieth wedding anniversary party. All the families of all the babies she had ever delivered were invited.

Dr. Kress winked at the photographer from the Washington *Star*. "Don't you need some boys in this picture?" said Dan, showing him the jolly handful of the Vechery twins. "Catch them quick, Bill, while they're still good-natured."

"That should be a good one," Bill countered. "Lead the way. Let's have one now with both of you doctors and all the children. Dr. Dan is as much at home with this circus as you are," the photographer told Lauretta.

"What a party! What a picture! What a story!" The reporter was having a good time, too. Joy and happiness walked with the doctors as they talked to their friends. Some of their guests were having a wonderful time, while others wept and wailed. Some were bored no end and sucked their pacifiers greedily; others longed for the next bottle.

It was a too-short two hours for the six hundred and more guests that afternoon. The golden moments were links in a chain of golden memories. Happiness, like a kiss, must be shared. Sharing was no new word for the Kresses—they could spell it in the dark backward. The day seemed a little empty after the noisy children had gone, but there were more activities for the Kresses' adult friends that evening.

From all over the globe they had been invited. Many sent letters and telegrams of greeting, which were read to the large group. Their many friends conferred an honorary degree upon the couple.

No mortarboards decorated their silvered hair. No flowing gowns of dignity inferred academic fulfillment. The degree was called L.L.D., which simply meant "Life Lovingly Dedicated."

Long after the last of the babies had been snuggled into his bed that night, the lanterns, colorful and gay, still burned on the Kresses' lawn. Their soft lights kept many happy memories burning. If all the good wishes given that day had been flowers, what a beautiful path they would have made into the future!

Hand in hand the Kresses stood in the doorway of their home after the guests had left. The gay lanterns no longer lighted the lawn. Now the moonlight filtered through the shadows of the trees.

Dan sighed. "What a day this has been!"

"Have we ever been happier?" Lauretta asked.

"No, I think not. You know, Etta, we've had a good life. I wouldn't change much of it if I could," Dan replied.

Etta laughed gaily. "When I think of Mr. Seventeen—well——"

Dan interrupted her thought. "Mr. Seventeen is now Mr. Seventy. How God led me to hate the things I once loved!"

Etta pressed his big hand a little tighter as she spoke. "I've been so proud of you, Daniel; and whatever we have accomplished, we have done it together."

"Hand in hand," Dan replied, smiling, "with God's help. And now there's a whole army of youth to take up the work as we lay it down."

Though these two devoted physicians had given more than fifty years of service to God and humanity, there was still a glowing future ahead of them. Ten years after the happy celebration of their fiftieth anniversary, they celebrated an even happier sixtieth.

Orlando, Florida, with its warm sunshine and refreshing tropical breezes became their home. Here a comfortable house, which they called "Mizpah," welcomed as always the many friends from all over the world who loved the dedicated doctors.

In the city of Orlando a church was built—The Kress Memorial Church. For years to come, young people would pause to reflect upon the lives of two Christian people who had been so devoted to the youth.

The work begun by Daniel and Lauretta Kress is still being carried on today. Though the torch has been passed to a new generation, the message of faith and hope still inspires young people everywhere.

Acknowledgments

The author gratefully acknowledges the assistance of these individuals: Grace Keith, who obtained many of the Kresses' personal manuscripts and papers; and Marie and Jens Neilsen, whose recollections of the Kresses' family life provided many interesting anecdotes.

Books and other material used for background:

The Home Physician and Guide to Health
Adventures in Medicine
The Doctors Mayo
Devils, Drugs and Doctors
The Lame, the Halt, the Blind
Behind the Doctor
Spirit of Prophecy books
Personal letters of Ellen G. White
Under the Guiding Hand,
the Kresses' own published diary